FOREWORD

I n recent months, several publications have made us increasingly aware of the dramatic shift southwards in Christian presence. The Christian majority has moved from being predominantly North American and European. Now, it is found in Asia, Africa, and Latin America as churches in the Southern Hemisphere experience explosive growth. Philip Jenkins has chronicled this growth in his recent book, *The Next Christendom: the Rise of Global Christianity,* and in several articles. Most of this growth, as Jenkins and others have noted, has a decidedly Pentecostal flavor, regardless of whether the churches are affiliated with Protestant denominations, the Catholic Church, or are independent of any denominational tradition. Many also have shed many of the traditions that reflect the cultural heritage of the churches of the North that planted them through the missionary movement. Instead, they have adapted their practices to indigenous cultures in their own setting.

In some respects these rapidly growing churches of the South have similarities to what Donald E. Miller called "new paradigm" churches in the United States—churches affiliated with such movements as the Vineyard Christian Fellowship, Calvary Chapel, and Hope Chapel. Miller analyzed these churches in his provocative book, *Reinventing Mainline Protestantism: Christianity in the New Millennium* (University of California Press, 1997). Fresh from that experience, he began a four-year study of rapidly growing churches in Asia, Africa, and Latin America. His particular focus in this new study has been on the way in which these Spirit-filled churches are also deeply engaged in social ministries in their communities. The full results of his work will be the subject of a forthcoming book, co-authored with Ted Yamamori and tentatively titled *Pentecostalism and Social Transformation: A Global Analysis,* also to be published by the University of California Press.

Knowing that Miller was engaged in this new study and aware of his insights into leadership in his earlier study of "new paradigm" churches in the United States, we asked him to reflect on what he was learning from his visits to these churches, especially on their leadership patterns. What might we, in the U.S., learn from them, especially in the way that they call forth, train, and exercise leadership? What follows is a description of these congregations and Miller's quite provocative personal reflections, both on patterns of church life that he encountered as well as leadership dynamics. His report takes the form more of a personal odyssey than a research paper. We believe readers will find it both challenging and stimulating.

To encourage further reflection on Miller's report, we have invited commentaries from Daniel Aleshire, Chad Hall, Grant Wacker, and William Willimon that are included in the report, each of whom brings his particular angle of vision to the topic.

Pulpit & Pew is a major project on pastoral leadership underway at Duke University Divinity School with generous funding from Lilly Endowment, Inc. In a variety of ways, Pulpit & Pew aims at providing answers to three broad sets of questions:

What is the state of pastoral leadership at the new century's beginning, and what do current trends portend for the next generation?

What is excellent ministry? Can we describe it? How does it come into being?

What can be done to enable excellent ministry to come into being more frequently, and how can it be nurtured and supported more effectively?

To learn more about Pulpit & Pew, we direct you to our Web site, www.pulpitandpew.duke.edu. You may also want to register to receive regular project updates from our electronic newsletter.

Jackson W Carroll

Jackson W. Carroll, Director
Pulpit & Pew: Research on Pastoral Leadership
Williams Professor Emeritus of Religion and Society

EXECUTIVE SUMMARY

The world of Christianity is being literally turned upside down, with a dramatic shift in locus from the Northern to the Southern hemisphere. Whereas a hundred years ago, 80 percent of Christians were either Europeans or North Americans, today 60 percent of all Christians live in Asia, Africa, and Latin America.

Undergoing dramatic growth, this emerging church in the "Two-Thirds World" is heavily Pentecostal, independent, non-denominational, very poor, and little understood by those in the Northern and Western Hemispheres.

For four years, Donald Miller spent two months each spring visiting dozens of rapidly growing Pentecostal and charismatic churches in 20 countries in the developing world. In this report, Miller reflects upon the leadership patterns he observed, convinced that North American Christians have much to learn from their fellow Christians in the Southern Hemisphere. The paper is part of a much broader research project Miller is conducting on fast-growing churches in the developing world with active social and community ministries.

Miller groups his conclusions on leadership around several themes, based upon characteristics he observed in the churches he visited:

- *Role of Vision*: The churches Miller studied all had visionary leaders who communicated their goals to a cadre of committed followers of Christ. Though they may lack seminary degrees or other formal training, these leaders approach life with an expectant spirit, believing that God will enter human history just as in scriptural accounts of the past.

- *Encounters with the "Mysterium Tremendum:"* Although it does not fit within the world view of most Westerners, leaders in these thriving churches in the developing world believe in a divine presence that is active in the universe and that can be and is encountered. They are convinced they are connected with the deepest truths and realities available to human beings.

- *Role of Worship*: Worship—both corporate and individual—is an essential element of leadership. The leaders in churches Miller visited spent considerable time each day in prayer, reflection, and meditation. Indeed, religious leadership that is disconnected from worship is impotent.

- *Organizing the People*: The most successful churches typically decentralized the ministry, affirming the Protestant principle of the priesthood of all believers. The clergy's job is to train people to do the work of ministry, rather than doing it themselves. Members are given substantial liberty to create new ministries and programs, subject to the pastor's control and direction. Churches typically employ a cell model of organization, which allows laity to develop leadership within a small group.

- *Social impact*: Pentecostal and charismatic churches in the developing world are merging their historical commitment to spirituality with a social transformation agenda that is creating innovative models of Christian social service and community organizing.

In a section entitled "A Few Further Elaborations," Miller discusses several implications of the leadership patterns he observed, particularly regarding the training of future leaders and the role of seminary education.

Miller concludes his report with "Some Immodest Proposals." He calls for U.S. churches to create mutual and equal relationships with churches in the developing world; restructuring seminaries based upon a series of proposed consultations between seminary leaders and the emergent church leaders; and sharing ideas and vision to help Christians around the world address social problems.

The report also contains four responses from Daniel Aleshire, director of the Association of Theological Schools; Chad Hall, pastor of Connection Church in Hickory, N.C.; Grant Wacker, professor of church history at Duke Divinity School, and William H. Willimon, professor of Christian ministry and dean of the chapel at Duke University.

INTRODUCTION

It had been three years since Ted Yamamori and I had visited Nairobi Chapel, located adjacent to Nairobi University in Kenya. On that Sunday morning, in spite of multiple services, the church was packed tight with 350 people inside the wood frame building, and another hundred sitting on benches outside. As part of our research project on global Pentecostalism, we had returned to interview Pastor Oscar Muriu to see what changes had occurred at the church since our last visit.

As we sat down in Oscar's comfortable study, we were told that the church had reached a ceiling in its growth. They now had seven services on a weekend, drawing about 2,500 adults. To deal with their over-crowded situation, the church had purchased 14 acres of land on the outskirts of Nairobi in an area where some of their members lived, and they were starting a new church that they expected would initially attract about a thousand people.

In 1999, when we had last visited Nairobi Chapel, they had a goal to start seven new churches by the year 2000. As they approached their goal at the turn of the millennium, the leadership of the church decided that this church planting strategy was much too slow. They needed to exercise more faith. Their new goal was to plant 300 churches by the year 2020, with the expectation that each of these churches would in turn plant daughter churches. Hence, within the next 20 years they hoped for 1,000 new congregations.

Although most of these churches were in Africa, Nairobi Chapel was in the process of planning their first church plant abroad—in Sidney, Australia. This church would not be for African immigrants. Rather, Oscar said that the Western world needs the spiritual vitality that the Two-Thirds World has to offer. In his view, churches in the West are working with a missionary model that is 50 years out of date. Christianity in the Southern Hemisphere is thriving. It is Europe, America, and countries such as Australia that need the Gospel.

When we asked Oscar how they were going to staff this ambitious program, he cited the example of Paul in Ephesians 4. The gifts of the spirit are given to equip the saints for service. He recited the philosophy articulated during our first visit to Nairobi Chapel. Every leader should be actively working to reproduce their gifts in another person. In his own case, he had established a timetable of seven years in which he would develop a leader who would take over his responsibilities at this church. Fortunately, he was able to cut this goal to four years, in part by regularly sharing the pulpit with emergent leaders within the church, which is why he was able to move to the new church they were establishing.

Much of their training of new leaders starts in a cell group of eight to 10 people, said Oscar. When the group grows to approximately 12, it is time for the cell to divide. When the split occurs, the apprentice to the

KENYA: Nairobi Pentecostal Church

leader now has the opportunity to lead his or her own group and, in time, to replicate their leadership with a new apprentice. It is in this small group setting that the real work of the church is done, including pastoral ministry, Bible study, and prayer. Sunday morning worship, said Oscar, is a time for celebration.

Cell groups are oftentimes involved in social ministries in their community. For example, we interviewed a mother of three children who started assisting women with AIDS. At first, this was her personal ministry, but within a few months the demand for services continued to increase. Thus she turned to the women in her cell group for assistance. Now they have a center that serves about 80 women, although it is bound to keep growing in size and scope. While the core leadership is from her cell group, it is expanding the ministry to include corporate sponsors and other sources of funding. Interestingly, although the center has a loose affiliation with Nairobi Chapel, no one is jealous to control it as a ministry of the church. Consequently, one of the key supporters is a pastor from another church in the local neighborhood.

Very few Nairobi Chapel leaders have seminary training, although most have university degrees. Oscar said that theological colleges are too expensive, take too long, and, unfortunately, remove students from the ongoing work of the church. Consequently, they have established their own church planting school. Drawing on the example of Jesus and Paul, mentoring and discipleship are the key strategies for creating new leaders, with the cell group being the primary laboratory for the initial phase of training. If the gifts of leadership are not manifest in this small group setting, it is highly unlikely that the individual will be able to lead an entire church—let alone plant new ones.

Since one of the criticisms of these fast-growing churches is that they emphasize spiritual transformation at the expense of social transformation, we inquired about the status of their social ministries. In particular, we were interested in the network of medical clinics they had established in the slums of Nairobi as part of their new church plants. In response to our question, Oscar said that they had reevaluated their strategy. As important as medical treatment seemed to them as outsiders when they entered these communities, according to Oscar medical treatment was not necessarily the priority of the residents. Sometimes the local population wanted a school or some other service.

KENYA: Nairobi Chapel vocational school

Consequently, now they go to the community leaders and ask them how this new church that they are establishing can best serve the neighborhood. They then work with the leadership to create a service that will be owned by the community, rather than imposed by the church on the community. In Oscar's words, "We have decided that we will let the community decide how they will facilitate these projects, because it gives them ownership of the service that we give to the community, and it lends credibility and authority to the church to be seen as representing the community and being part of the community."

We were also interested in the progress being made by a group of Nairobi Chapel members who had formed a group called "Christians for a Just Society." Three years previously they had published a white paper on political corruption. This seemed to be a bold move, since it was critical of government policy. Recently, said Oscar, because of the group's forthright leadership, they have been asked to serve as the secretariat to all the Non-Governmental Organizations in Kenya that are monitoring political elections. Hence, people outside of the church are recognizing the group's integrity as well as their servant leadership. In addition, Christians for a Just Society has established a mentoring program for young politicians who are entering public service, linking them with older Christian politicians. Oscar said that this group is trying to instill in these politicians a commitment to the biblical standards of justice, "a sense of responsibility and duty to the populace, and a commitment to be men and women of integrity."

Nairobi Chapel has established another innovative program. Working with the youth and parents of the church, the church has created a rite of passage to assist young people in the difficult transition to adulthood. In Oscar's view, modernity has destroyed the initiation rites that were an important element of African culture. To compensate for this void, the church has designed a new set of initiation rites for youth as they enter puberty. While it is no longer possible for a teenage boy to kill a lion to demonstrate his readiness to be a man, nor is it morally right for young women to undergo female circumcision, there are other experiences that can symbolize the transition to adulthood. At the conclusion of these ritual experiences, parents from the church join their children to write a contract regarding new responsibilities and liberties that they will have as young adults.

THE NEW FOCUS OF CHRISTIANITY

Since its inception in the first century, Christianity has been evolving as a social institution, changing its organizational shape, redefining its mission, and creating new expressions of worship. Perhaps the rate of change is no greater in the 21st century than at other periods in the church's history, but from my experience of traveling internationally during the past few years, it appears as if the world of Christianity is being turned upside down. And I mean this quite literally.

In 1900, 80 percent of Christians were either Europeans or North Americans, states David Barrett and his colleagues in the *World Encyclopedia of Christianity*.[1] Today, 60 percent of all Christians live in Asia, Africa, or Latin America. The momentum of Christianity has moved to the Southern Hemisphere. The colonial notion of Christianizing "heathens" through heroic missionary activity is something of an anachronism. The tables have turned. Churches in Asia, Africa and Latin America are now sending missionaries to the West, believing that they have a message from the Christian gospel to share with secular Europe and America. Philip Jenkins states, "the phrase 'a white Christian' may sound like a curious oxymoron," projecting that by the middle of this century only one-fifth of the world's three billion Christians will be non-Hispanic whites.[2]

There are two other demographic revolutions brewing that will change the face of Christianity. According to Barrett, 26 percent of Christians globally are what can be called Pentecostal, including 30 percent of Christians in the United States. British sociologist, David Martin, calls the growth of Pentecostalism "the largest global shift in the religious marketplace over the last 40 years."[3] He conservatively estimates Pentecostalism at a quarter of a billion people and says that while it was initially a lower class phenomenon, it is increasingly drawing middle income people.

Pentecostalism takes its name from the experience of Jesus' disciples on the day of Pentecost, described in Acts 2:4, "when they were all filled with the Holy Spirit and began to speak in other tongues, as the Spirit gave them utterance." Worldwide, Pentecostalism takes many forms—for example both as organized denominations and independent churches, but the movement is distinguished by an emphasis on the experience of the "baptism of the Spirit," often, but not always, evidenced by speaking in tongues. Pentecostals are also typically quite conservative in their theology. Related to Pentecostalism and often referred to as "neo-Pentecostalism" is the charismatic movement. This movement shares some of Pentecostalism's enthusiasm and emphasis on spiritual experience, but it is typically a movement within established, non-Pentecostal denominations and churches aimed at revitalizing them from within. Most of the congregations that I describe here are

[1] David B. Barrett, George T. Kurian and Todd M. Johnson, *World Christian Encyclopedia*, 2nd ed (New York: Oxford University Press, 2001, pp. 3-23.

[2] Philip Jenkins, *The Next Christendom: The Coming of Global Christianity* (Oxford: Oxford University Press, 2002), p. 3.

[3] David Martin, *Pentecostalism: The World Their Parish* (Oxford: Blackwell, 2002), p. xvii.

self-consciously Pentecostal and are often independent of denominational affiliation. Some, however, are more accurately called charismatic. All of them, however, give strong emphasis to the work of the Holy Spirit and to the believer's direct spiritual experience.

A dramatic shift is also occurring in the organizational form of the Christian church. Globally, according to Barrett's research, 20 percent of Christians are members of independent churches, up from 8 percent in 1970.[4] Some of these churches are splits from less progressive denominations. Other independent churches have been started by religious entrepreneurs who have a vision for sharing the good news of Christianity with non-churched people and consequently are utilizing non-conventional expressions of worship and organizational management. Denominations have gained a reputation for being hierarchical, authoritarian, and slow to understand the changing cultural realities of our postmodern world. Consequently, tens of thousands of new churches have formed in the last several decades that are linked together in networks, founded on relationships rather than denominational ties.

"Liberation theology opted for the poor, and the poor opted for Pentecostalism."

I am a member of an Episcopal congregation in the United States, and the reality of this demographic shift came home to me when I examined the profile of the Anglican Communion to which The Episcopal Church belongs. Currently, 53 percent of Anglicans reside in Africa, far outstripping the next largest region, namely Europe, which claims a third of all Anglicans. The contrast is dramatized when one realizes that Nigeria has seven times more Anglicans than the United States. Furthermore, many elements of the Anglican Communion have a charismatic flair, or, alternatively, worship in a far more exuberant style than does the typical Episcopalian in the United States.

The Anglican Communion is not alone in this realignment of its membership. The same thing is happening within Catholicism, whose next pontifical leader may, indeed, come from the Southern Hemisphere. There are also significant elements of the Catholic Church that are charismatic, embracing the gifts of the Spirit. In Manila, for example, I witnessed several hundred

thousands of Catholics gathering every Saturday night in an open field, singing choruses, holding their hands to the darkened sky in praise, and seeking miracles of body and financial well being. In Sao Paulo, Brazil, I visited a dynamic Catholic Church of several thousand Spirit-filled people who were utilizing Pentecostal hymns from a decade ago. In Hyderbad, India, I went to a huge Catholic Charismatic retreat center that draws tens of thousands of pilgrims each year for weeklong retreats.

This same process is occurring within other Protestant churches. In Addis Ababa, Ethiopia, for example, I asked the head of the church council if any of the mainline denominations had charismatic elements, and he laughed and said they are all Spirit-filled, including the Presbyterians. While theologian Harvey Cox explains the growth of Pentecostalism and the charismatic movement in terms of an "ecstasy deficit" in contemporary culture, there are many competing hypotheses. Those within the Pentecostal tradition see the growth as a fresh outpouring of the Holy Spirit for our age, while some social theorists view this movement as an inevitable part of the cycle of renewing moribund denominational structures. When I asked one well-informed theologian in South America why Pentecostalism was growing while liberation theology, for example, seems to be declining, he replied succinctly: "Liberation theology opted for the poor, and the poor opted for Pentecostalism." In his view, progressive politics can never substitute for deep spiritual engagement, although the two can go hand-in-hand—which is the argument that Ted Yamamori and I make based on our research.

With this change in the population base of Christianity, there is also a dramatic shift in the socio-economic characteristics of the Christian Church. In contrast to the western Church, which is considerably relatively affluent, global Christianity is made up mostly of the poor. In many ways, this should not be surprising, especially if one looks at global statistics: Over half of the world's population live a precarious existence, and nearly one-fifth are desperately poor. When these Christians worship, they come to God with different concerns than do their North American and European counterparts, and this affects their style of worship. They are oftentimes less cerebral in their worship. They have a different attitude towards the miraculous. And they are sometimes more conserva-

---

[4]   Barrett, p. 10.

tive in their theology and moral views, offending the sensibilities of Enlightenment-saturated Western Christians. I went, for example, to a three-and-a-half-hour worship service in a township in Johannesburg, South Africa. Although that may seem a little excessive by Western standards—where the sermon is allocated 12 minutes and everything is timed so the service ends in an hour and 15 minutes—this South African congregation broke for lunch after morning worship and then reconvened at 3 p.m. for the next installment of praise and healing.

There is also a failure by many Western Christians to understand the sexual and gender mores of Christians in the Southern Hemisphere, as well as other cultural differences. Many of us have no appreciation of animism, no experiential understanding of poverty, and little comprehension of cultures that are based on collective rather than individualistic values. While Western values have much to recommend them—especially the emphasis on democratic governance—we need to understand better the cultural context in which the new face of Christendom is being expressed. When we do, our attitudes towards certain practices by Southern Hemisphere Christians may be less strident.

A Personal Pilgrimage

A decade ago I ventured out from the safety of my liberal Episcopal Church in Pasadena, California, to visit a network of "new paradigm" churches that started in response to the cultural changes initiated in the 1960s. My research odyssey in these neo-Pentecostal churches is described in *Reinventing American Protestantism*, where I argue that a second reformation of sorts is occurring—this time focused on the "medium" of Christianity rather than the "message" of the Christian faith.[5] While I never felt tempted to join one of these churches that I was studying, I did undergo a profound shift in my worldview when I realized that I was trapped in an Enlightenment ideology that privileged mind over body and perpetuated a dualistic epistemology that many of the postmodern members of new paradigm churches had long ago abandoned.

After publication of this book, I noticed that many of my fellow liberals began to shun me, and there were

members of the academy who thought I had lost my mind. Indeed, I confess to having somewhat overstated my thesis, because I intended the book to be a wake-up call for the declining mainline churches. I could, of course, have written a cynical critique of these churches that were experimenting with new worship styles and forms of social organization, but that would have simply reinforced the stereotypes that comfort many liberal Christians as they watch their church populations age and decline in membership. Nevertheless, there was a glaring inadequacy in the research for this book: I did not fully explore the social ministries of these churches. Were they making any difference within their communities? Did they understand the Great Commandment to love others as much as yourself, or were they one-sided in their fixation on the Great Commission to save the world? Also, how were these churches responding to the Old Testament mandates related to justice, care of widows, orphans, and the poor in one's midst?

In 1998, I was invited to a consultation in the Philippines that was hosted by Tetsunao (Ted) Yamamori, president of Food for the Hungry, to discuss a book that he was editing on the response of Christians to poverty in urban cities around the world. At the end of the meeting we were relaxing over dinner in a Manila restaurant when the topic turned to future research projects, and the idea occurred to us that we might test the argument of *Reinventing American Protestantism* on a global scale, but this time we would focus on the social ministries of these churches.

PHILLIPINES: Jesus is Lord Church, Manila

---

[5] Donald E. Miller, *Reinventing American Protestantism: Christianity in the New Millennium* (Berkeley: University of California Press, 1997.)

After securing a generous travel grant from a foundation that had previously funded both of us, Fieldstead and Company, we sent letters to over 300 church leaders, missiologists, and scholars asking them to suggest congregations that fit these four stipulations:

- They were located in the developing world;

- They were experiencing rapid growth;

- They were self-funding, rather than supported by outside mission agencies;

- And, most importantly, they were deeply involved in social ministries within their communities.

To our surprise, 85 percent of the nominations for case studies turned out to be Pentecostal or, at least, charismatic. Consequently, Yamamori and I spent approximately two months each spring for the next four years traveling around the globe studying Pentecostal and charismatic churches that fit the foregoing criteria. We visited 20 different countries and conducted interviews with nearly 400 individuals. Some Sundays we attended three or four difference church services. We also wrote field notes on dozens of different churches and their social ministries.

It is important to note that, although these congregations were selected as a result of a nomination process, they are not representative of all Two-Thirds World churches. Many churches in the developing world are quite small and struggling, often like "storefront" churches in the U. S.; many are not Pentecostal or

PHILLIPINES: Jesus is Lord Church, Manila

charismatic; and many are not as socially active and engaged as those described here. The churches we studied are *not* representative of all churches in the developing world. They were chosen to fit specific criteria, especially fast growing churches that are committed to meeting the social needs of people in their communities. The phenomenon of socially engaged Pentecostal churches is relatively new, often a decade or less in development, but I am convinced that this focus on the "holistic gospel" is gradually replacing more legalistic expressions of traditional Pentecostalism.

Cutting across all of these churches we studied are some common themes that we observed about their leadership, organization, and practices. Since I am not a consultant on church growth, I am not advocating adopting these strategies; rather, my intention is more modest: namely, to offer some generalizations about ways in which Christians around the globe are seeking to be faithful to their identity as followers of Christ. What follows then are observations and personal reflections based on my experiences rather than systematic research findings. These reflections have led me to ask whether and how what I have observed might apply to U.S. churches and their leaders. Before turning to these observations, however, I state my own strong negative view of the stereotypes that some North American Protestants (including some North American evangelicals) have of these churches in the Southern Hemisphere, because many of the churches are Pentecostal or charismatic in form.

For one thing, it is unfair for Protestants in North America to superimpose stereotypical images of televangelists on Christians in the developing world and then marginalize them as unsophisticated, culturally retrograde animists who are engaged in superstitious behaviors that compensate for their deprived social circumstances. It is quite possible that God acts in miraculous ways on behalf of people who have no recourse to antibiotics and modern medicine. In addition, it is also possible that many people who involve their body as well as mind in worship may have escaped certain limitations of the modernist worldview. Indeed, they may actually be more holistic in their mentality than Western Christians who are trapped in an Enlightenment worldview. Finally, many of these Christians may have a better understanding of what it means to be a selfless servant of Christ than do Westerners who are surrounded by the conveniences of modern society.

By making such suggestions, I do not wish to romanticize the poor, nor am I arguing that there are not pathologies inherent in some practices—for example, emphasizing faith-healing as a cure for AIDS patients. At the same time, I am convinced that we in North America have a great deal to learn from our fellow Christians in the developing world, and I also believe that local churches in the U.S. should create partnerships with churches in the Southern Hemisphere in order to engage in mutual learning and collaboration. By so doing, we will open ourselves to what God is doing in the world and may thereby discover our role in being God's hands and feet to the poor, marginalized, and afflicted—as described in Matthew 25.

After every trip that I have made to churches in the developing world I have come back humbled by my own lack of faith, my own failure of imagination, and my resistance to commit myself to the high standard of being a servant of Christ. We in North America live in a bubble of affluence and convenience, and this affects our theology. Again, I'm not romanticizing poverty and implying that poor Christians are inherently more spiritual than wealthy Christians. Rather, confronting poverty on a daily basis—or religious persecution, or manifestations of the demonic—creates concrete occasions to test whether the Christian faith works. And when it does, the context is created for faith development of leaders who are called to serve with great vision and purpose.

THE ROLE OF VISION

All of the vital churches that Yamamori and I have studied are marked by visionary leaders who have communicated their goals to a cadre of committed followers of Christ, many being relatively recent converts. Formal training for the task of leadership has little to do with their success. In fact, many times they do not possess seminary degrees. Instead, they have had a radical, life-changing encounter with God, and have subsequently become voracious readers of scripture—trying to practice the demands of the gospel, often quite literally—while simultaneously borrowing organizational ideas from whatever source they can find, including their own imagination. These leaders approach everyday life with an expectant spirit, believing that God will enter human history in the same way that the scriptures reveal the acts of God in the past.

Many of these leaders also take prayer and meditation very seriously, both corporately and personally. All night prayer meetings are very common in Africa, but I have also encountered them in Latin America. These meetings typically start around 10 p.m. and go until 6 a.m. the next day. During this time there is singing, preaching, laying on of hands, as well as hours of praising God and calling on him for help. One of my most poignant recollections is of a group of young people in a barrio in Caracas, Venezuela. A woman whose son had been killed through gang violence started the group. Rather than retreating into bitterness and rage, she opened her very modest home to the youth of the neighborhood. Every Friday night she crowds 30 to 40 kids into her dining room and a small adjacent room where they sing, dance, testify, and preach. There are no guitars, just one youth who is drumming on an overturned and empty tin food container. In some ways, there is a nearly orgiastic quality to the gathering. But this exuberance is complemented by what appears to be a sincere desire to seek the face of Christ, to forego sexual temptation, and to commit oneself to a life worthy of a child of God.

When mainline (and many evangelical) Protestants think of Pentecostals, they often imagine people speaking in tongues, falling down as they are slain in the spirit, or throwing away crutches as they hobble across a stage. While these things happen—for example, recently, while videotaping a Johannesburg church service, I was knocked off my feet and into a nearby chair as a large man fell under the power of the Spirit—this exuberance is not found in many of the growing neo-Pentecostal churches. There the presence of the Holy Spirit is often more subtle, less dramatic, and in some ways more profound. In short, vital Spirit-filled churches are characterized by pastors and people who open themselves to the presence of the Holy Spirit for guidance. Sometimes unusual things happen: God speaks to them in dreams, visions, or prophecy. More often, however, they have insights, growing convictions, or an emergent desire to push beyond the comfort zone of everyday life. Stated differently, when people are open to the possibility, the Holy Spirit seems to challenge self-interest and complacency and nudge them into doing the heroic, even the unimaginable. In fact, I have often been tempted to think: "These people are megalomaniacs." And then I discover that, indeed, they did start five new churches last year; open a medical clinic; now have three new nursery schools in impoverished communities; and so on.

How do they accomplish such grandiose visions? Every example has its own story, but it is possible to generalize to some degree. First, these faithful Christians are inordinately self-sacrificing and dedicated. They do not believe that they own their lives; instead, they have given them to God for his service. Second, they worship ecstatically together and in this process the Spirit refreshes them. They are not running on their own power or they would be constantly exhausted. Third, they have deep meditative lives and in these quiet times invite the Holy Spirit to renew them, inspire them, lead them. Indeed, if they were operating on their own desire or commitment, they would burn out after a few months or years. Fourth, they often build strong organizational structures. It would be a serious mistake to think that their projects and programs run solely on Holy Spirit hoopla. On the other hand, without the Holy Spirit their efforts would result in pedantic organizations reflecting the visionary's egoistic ambitions, not the spirit of a compassionate God.

ENCOUNTERS WITH THE *MYSTERIUM TREMENDUM*

The Christian project doesn't work unless there is a divine presence active in the universe. For millennia, this presence has been called the Holy Spirit by Christ followers. The story told in the Book of Acts is that Jesus left behind the comforter, the Holy Spirit, when he ascended into heaven. Personally, I'm not very attached to the three-tiered universe idea of heaven above, hell beneath, and the in-between world of struggling humans pulled this way and that by opposing forces. Indeed, contemporary astronomy has catapulted us a long ways from this simplistic rendering of cosmic reality. At the same time, I'm convinced that the Christian project continues because people encounter the presence of the Holy Spirit in their lives. Without this manifestation of the Spirit, we have empty organizational forms—which, of course, describes some manifestations of the Christian church.

Within my own Anglican tradition, there has been a strong emphasis on the "trinity" of *tradition, reason, and scripture* as a means for knowing God's will. This formula dates back to the late 16th and early 17th centuries where first John Jewel and then Richard Hooker used the formula to do battle with both Catholics, who ignored scripture, and Protestants,

PHILLIPINES: El Shaddai, charismatic Catholic sect, Manila

who emphasized scripture at the expense of reason and tradition. While there is much to be commended by this balanced approach—for example, I find myself strongly attracted to the rhythm of the liturgy and the emphasis on reason and scientific investigation—there is also something missing that the Wesleyan tradition added to its Anglican forebears: namely *experience*.

It is not that Anglicans are devoid of religious experience. In many ways, for example, I find the Anglican liturgy capable of fostering a mystical encounter with what Rudolf Otto called the *mysterium tremendum*. But our sophistication and emphasis on order and decorum tend to strip us of a vocabulary for talking about such spiritual encounters. Consequently, there is often fear and even hostility expressed towards those who talk too openly about experiences. One explanation of this fear, of course, is that acknowledging the right to personal revelation threatens the authority of the priestly class. But that interpretation is too cynical. A more plausible explanation is that we reject divine encounter because it does not fit our worldview, or at least the worldview of the educated elite of our society who chose to dichotomize mind and body, flesh and spirit, mythology and truth.

I believe that we need to move beyond these dichotomies if the Christian church is going to have vitality, even if doing so makes liberal Christians like me nervous. I have encountered in Asia, Africa and Latin America a number of phenomena that do not fit the Western liberal worldview. In India, for example, Ted Yamamori and I interviewed a young woman who even her fellow Hindu villagers claimed had died and was raised from the dead by the prayers of two devout Christians. In Hong Kong, we did extensive interviews with heroin drug addicts who met Jesus, then received the Holy Spirit, and during the next week went through painless withdrawal. In Brazil, we witnessed demons being cast out of possessed individuals, and these individuals were subsequently liberated from external forces that had controlled their behavior. And everywhere we traveled there were numerous accounts offered of supernatural healings.

At one level, I try to maintain a skeptical attitude towards these claims—a product of spending years reading Marx, Freud, and other debunkers of reli-

gious enthusiasm. On the other hand, I have opened my worldview wide enough to allow for the possibility of the supernatural. In fact, on a one-week silent retreat to commemorate my 50th birthday, I had an encounter with the demonic that, while subject to various interpretations, made me acutely aware that reality may not be what Western rationalists always perceive it to be. Hence, it is possible that the miracles performed by Jesus and his disciples are still occurring in the 21st century—at least for those who have eyes to see and ears to hear. At the same time, one must always test these experiences by the other three sources of knowledge of God—scripture, tradition, and reason.

For me, one of the great revelations that has emerged from interviewing hundreds of Pentecostals is the discovery that these individuals are typically bright, articulate, reasoning human beings who happen to believe in divine encounters. William James' analysis of the *Varieties of Religious Experience*, which I had read in graduate school, provided me a philosophical foundation for critiquing reductionistic models—what James calls "medical materialism." Nevertheless, it sometimes requires "encounters of a close kind" to turn intellectual formulations into experiential truths.[6] Cynics, of course, will claim that I have "gone native" after a decade of hanging around Pentecostals. That is one possible reading, but a more charitable interpretation is that I am making a transition out of the ideology of modernism, which, admittedly, is a one-dimensional world.

Recently, while in a Singapore bookstore, I read a good portion of Bishop John Shelby Spong's attempt to liberate Christianity from the "primitivism" of the biblical worldview.[7] During my graduate school days, this book would have electrified me, as did John Robinson's *Honest to God*, which I read in the mid-1960s. Frankly, however, Spong's book bored me after a while, primarily because it was so predictable and also because it was long on critique and short on creative solutions to the mysteries of the Spirit. In contrast, I have found the work of Marcus Borg to be much more exciting, because he seems to recognize the validity of the supernatural elements of Jesus' shamanistic practices. Jesus and the early leaders of

[6] See William James, *The Varieties of Religious Experience: A Study in Human Nature* (New York: Collier Books, 1961).

[7] John Shelby Spong, *A New Christianity for a New World: Why Traditional Faith Is Dying and How a New Faith Is Being Born* (HarperSanFrancisco, 2001).

Christianity understood the supernatural, and they unapologetically healed people, cast out demons, and multiplied bread and fishes.

I clearly acknowledge the potential for abuse and even greed by Christian miracle workers, many of whom are far from self-critical about their work. Various claims about God's miracles need to be tested and critiqued. I agree, for example, with the critique by Oscar Muriu, Nairobi Chapel's pastor, of what are often called "health and wealth" churches in Africa—those that promise both health and worldly success to people who join their ministries. Such churches are growing, Muriu believes, because they make unrealistic promises to people who are desperately poor. Their pledge that faith in God will bring about an easy and quick change in their life circumstances is extraordinarily attractive, but it runs counter to scripture, tradition, reason, and the experience of God's people. Nevertheless, to reject outright all such claims about the manifestations of God's Spirit in the world—whether promising health and wealth or some other spiritual gift—as "abuses of Christian teaching" is not only specious logic. It also blinds one to seeing how God's Spirit is at work in people's lives in often complex and demanding ways.

> *On a daily basis people commune with God; they seek God's presence; they await divine instructions.*

What gives power to the leaders of these churches, pastors and laity alike, is the conviction that they are connected with the deepest truths and realities available to the human species. This truth is not the result of deductive reasoning; it is experientially based. On a daily basis people commune with God; they seek God's presence; they await divine instructions. No longer are their lives the result merely of strategic calculation intended to fulfill their personal desires and ambitions. They have been called to a life of service. Their fundamental task as a servant-leader is to perceive what God wants done in the world and then to carry out this divine plan, not with one's own strength but, quite literally, with the power of God.

Some of the most significant ministries I have observed are not led by individuals with "big personalities." Quite the opposite, they are oftentimes unas-suming individuals. Take Maggie Gobran, for example. She was raised in a wealthy family in Cairo, Egypt, and as a married woman lived the life of a well-heeled socialite. One day, however, she encountered a desperately poor woman selling a few items as a way of supporting her family. Maggie looked into the eyes of this woman and her young daughter and saw herself and her own daughter Anne—except for the grace of God. This encounter led her into the slums of Cairo, where people make their living by sorting garbage. The stench made her sick for several days after her first visit, but she kept going back, because increasingly she did not see herself or her daughter in these poor families. Instead, she told us that she saw the presence of Christ in the eyes of these children, and that by caring for them she was physically touching Christ. Now Momma Maggie, as the children call her, has established a network of approximately 30 nursery schools for children in these slums. She also has started a vocational school for youth who cannot attend school. And several thousand children each year attend summer camps, where they are able to eat as much food as they want. They are also taught hygiene, moral values, and, most importantly, they are told they are valued because God loves them.

Maggie Gobran is a quiet, self-effacing woman. In the place of ego, there appears to be the spirit of Christ. The people working with her radiate this same spirit of compassion and vitality. What energizes this work is clearly not the desire for fame—believe me, this would not be a sufficient basis to sustain one in entering the slums of Cairo on a daily basis. Rather, Maggie believes that God has called her into a life of service, as is also the case with many other servant-leaders whose lives have been marked by the experience of being *called* rather than by a self-appointed vocational ambition.

THE ROLE OF WORSHIP

In the literature I have read, leadership is seldom, if ever, connected to worship. Yet, what seems most to sustain servant-leaders in these congregations is the act of worship, both individual and corporate. Every one of the exemplary leaders that I met spends considerable time each day in prayer, reflection, and meditation. This quiet period of the day is when the Spirit seems to speak to them, giving them direction and correction, new ideas, and insights into the potential, as well as vices and frailties, of people they will encounter that day. Moreover, a worshipping community of people who collectively have the resources to energize a prophetic presence in the world also sustains these exemplary leaders.

In thinking about the failure of liberation theology, whose social critique I admire, I believe that it was unsustainable in many contexts because it did not sufficiently emphasize the importance of nurturing a strong worshipping community—which is the basis for sustaining a life of empowered commitment. In collective worship, several important things transpire. First is acknowledgement of the source of life through various means of celebration and commemoration. Singing is the nearly universal means of collective expression, and this is most powerful when done in the local parlance rather than imitating another culture's musical idiom. Second, Christian worship has moments of self-examination, followed by penance and requests for forgiveness. This is done through prayers, collects (in liturgical churches), and public confession. Third, there is a period for teaching, which may include recitation of the roots of the Christian tradition through reading of sacred texts, remembrance of saints from the heritage, and commentary on scripture that is followed by moral and spiritual exhortation. Fourth is the opportunity for people to gather around the table, remembering the words and acts of Jesus during his last meal with his disciples, connecting with the symbol—or mystical reality, depending on the tradition—of Christ's body and blood. It is these elements of worship that renew individuals, give them vision and power, while at the same time connecting them to a community of people who can work collectively to bring God's justice and compassion to a broken world.

Drawing on sociological theory, one can argue that religious leadership that is disconnected from worship is impotent. Not only is worship essential to sustaining the moral order of a community of people, but as the sociologist Emile Durkheim has aptly stated, at the heart of every good ritual are moments of collective effervescence in which individual identity is fused with collective purpose. While Durkheim reduced these moments of animation to purely social origin (i.e., celebration of the community's collective conscience which is greater than any single individual), the

Christian faith rests on the premise that the "something more" than Durkheim acknowledged is the Creator God to whom we owe our being. Hence, worship is an essential element of the triangulation whereby the leader, community, and God become partners in a collaborative enterprise. In worship God gives us the inspiration and power to be his agents in the world; in worship we experience the unity of purpose that undergirds our collective activity as the people of God; and in worship we are given direction by individuals whom God has called to be his servant-leaders. All of this makes sense, however, only if there is a God who elects to act in this world through human beings as an expression of his creative initiative.

One of the things that surprised me the most when I started studying new paradigm churches was how much time they spent singing. They did not refer to this extended period as "singing," but as "worship." Furthermore, their songs were quite different from the hymns sung in my own church tradition. The hymns to which I was accustomed often contained "meaty" theology; the new paradigm church songs were mostly simple chorus with highly repetitive lyrics. Also, another substantial difference is that traditional hymns are often statements *about* God or Christ, while the new paradigm worshippers are singing directly *to* God or Jesus. While I was trying to sort out this puzzle, one of my interviewees put it simply: "The difference," she said, "is writing a letter *to* someone you love compared to writing *about* someone for whom you care."

The other difference between the two styles of worship is the use of contemporary musical instruments.

UGANDA: Kampala Pentecostal worship

New paradigm churches almost never have organs or even pianos. Depending on the country, guitars, keyboard, drums, saxophones and/or various brass instruments are standard fare. In poor and undeveloped countries, there may be no accompaniment or perhaps a simple padded mitt that is struck to keep time to the music. There are also substantial differences in sound systems. In Singapore I attended a church in a newly constructed auditorium that had an incredible projection screen resembling a gigantic television screen, along with a million dollars of television recording equipment. It also had a sound system to rival that used in any rock concert. On the other hand, we visited a church in Hyderabad, India, that had only a few drummers. In the middle of the service, we all left the church building and walked a quarter mile into a rice field where there was a water cistern. There a half dozen new converts were baptized in full immersion with their clothes clinging to them. The Singapore church with its sophisticated equipment did not seem to me have exhibited greater spiritual fervor or depth in its worship than in the rural church in India. Rather, different contexts necessitated different worship styles and accoutrements.

What seems to be common to vital worshipping communities is warmth among the members. People talk with each other, hug, embrace, and kiss. There is often a sweetness in the air that can only be felt and not described. My speculation is that it comes from people being willing to yield themselves to the Spirit and thus experience God in relationships with one another and let a spirit of gentleness and humility take over. Perhaps, not surprisingly, there is often an acknowledgement in these worship services of brokenness and helplessness, and an acknowledgement that one's strength comes only from Christ. In such worship, the worship leader is more like Max Weber's notion of the charismatic leader as a *vessel* of the divine, rather than the more popular view of the charismatic leader as a dynamic extrovert who leads by force of personality.

ORGANIZING THE PEOPLE

Visionary leadership is essential to a vital, healthy, growing church. But that does not mean that the clerical staff does all the work. Quite the contrary, the most successful churches typically decentralize the ministry, affirming the Protestant

BRAZIL: March for Jesus

principle of the priesthood of all believers. The job of the clergy involves training the people to do the work of ministry rather than the clergy doing it themselves. For this model to work, the people must have a relatively high level of biblical literacy. Otherwise the content that fires the ministry is absent. It is also important that the senior pastor of the congregation maintain veto power over any "craziness" that might get implemented by fervent members whose vision needs moderating or rechanneling. This said, however, there is substantial liberty given to members to create new ministries and develop programs. Without this permission, new paradigm churches would not be nearly so innovative and entrepreneurial. At the same time, the senior pastor still maintains considerable control, because he or she defines the overall vision and also, as mentioned, has veto power over the proposed new ministries or programs.

Some type of a cell-based church—for example, the one in Nairobi that I described previously—seems to be the model that works best in these churches. Such a model makes it possible for laity to develop leadership skills within a small group setting. Furthermore, the cell model relieves the clergy in large churches of ministering to the individual needs of thousands of people. Instead, this is primarily done at the cell group level, with the lay leader of the cell group having access to more senior leaders in the event of a problem that he or she cannot handle. Clearly, however, the frontline of ministry is always at the cell group level.

Various theories exist about what constitutes the most effective cell group structure and practice. To give but a few examples, some argue for homogeneous cell groups made up of people from the same profession, class, or who share common interests. Others argue for multigenerational cell groups that include young and old alike. Still other theories restrict the content of the cell group meeting, suggesting that cell groups should discuss the pastor's sermon of the previous week, while other others believe in a degree of autonomy for leaders, where they select the theme or text for discussion.

When the cell-oriented church is Pentecostal or charismatic, the gifts of the Spirit are often manifest within the cell meeting, with members praying for healing, prophesying, or speaking in tongues. In some instances, relegating the gifts of the Spirit to the cell group is a way of "sanitizing" the larger worship meeting for unchurched people who might be offended by such dramatic displays of healing or prophecy. On the other hand, it is precisely the tenderness of praying for someone in a small group setting that may be appealing. One interviewee told me that her cell group was like an extended family, caring for her in a way that her biological family never did. After all, within healthy family settings people are touched, hugged, worried over, and prayed for, and it is precisely this intimacy that is missing for many people living in urban settings, whether in the West or in the developing world.

Undoubtedly, different approaches are appropriate for different contexts, and I will not argue for one methodology over another except to suggest that the cell group strategy seems to work well if the entire church is structured around such groups. Experience has often shown, however, that shortly after this change is initiated, many churches take a short-term "nose-dive" because the authority of those in traditional roles is altered, and some people become alienated and leave. Gone are 90 percent of the committee meetings as well as guilds and other ensconced organizations. After this initial downturn, many churches then experience a long-term period of growth because the cell group model permits many more people to be actively involved and hold leadership roles. Furthermore, properly functioning cell groups become tools of evangelism because of their permeability. Cell groups often take responsibility for serving non-Christians in their immediate neighborhood, and members also invite their friends to join them in these informal home settings, which for many people are less intimidating than entering a church building.

In Manila, I witnessed the linkage between cell groups and evangelism at a large Sunday evening gathering of 5,000 or so people. After a song or two, an invitation was given for people to come forward to acknowledge their birth as new Christians. The timing of this altar call did not make any sense to me until someone whispered in my ear that the hundred people who had come to the stage had all become Christians that week in their cell groups, and now they were giving witness to their conversion before the larger body of Christ. The end of the service—typically the time for an altar call—was reserved instead for Christians who came forward for prayer and healing.

Although cell group advocates typically argue that they are modeling this organizational structure after the first-century church, it should be recognized that the cell approach is essentially a coping strategy for large, ever expanding churches that, nevertheless, do have historical precedents.[8] These churches with multiple thousands could never hire enough clergy to keep up with the demand for pastoral ministry. The cells also serve as a strategy for new church planting and leadership development. One starts by developing a cell group with the intentional goal of multiplying it. A few believers invite their non-Christian neighbors and friends into their home for a time of Bible study, prayer, and fellowship. Sometimes these cells grow into churches. Sometimes they languish. A wise and experienced leader of a movement told me that you measure leadership—and whether one is called to be a pastor—by whether a cell group led by a particular individual stagnates or grows.

The problem with foreign money is that it creates dependency, which is precisely the opposite of building self-sufficient indigenous leadership.

The structure of these gatherings seems to follow the same format, regardless of the teaching style. First, there is an "ice-breaker" where people share something about themselves or what is going on in their lives. This is followed by a brief worship time, accompanied by someone playing guitar, if there is appropriate talent available in the group. Next is a period of Bible study and discussion, which is often followed by a time of prayer for people with special needs. Finally, there are light refreshments. In addition to this formal structure, various activities may be associated with cell groups. For example, if someone has lost a job or there is a medical need in the family, the cell group members may pitch in to help this individual. Cell groups may also do informal outings as families, and, as previously mentioned, they may pursue various social ministries within their community.

Beyond the emphasis on cell groups, there are other organizational innovations that characterize these churches. For example, although many are focused on missions and new church planting, there is a growing movement to use the medium of business as a way of gaining access to countries that are not hospitable to Christianity. My colleague Ted Yamamori calls these individuals "holistic entrepreneurs," and has been compiling examples of people who have established businesses in other countries with the explicit goal of then starting a church or underground fellowship of Christians. These individuals are self-supporting, and, in fact, the integrity of their business activity requires that it eventually turns a profit.

Another organizational characteristic that I encountered within the developing world is a suspicion of foreign mission money as an advanced form of colonialism. While it may only cost a few thousand dollars to construct a church or fund a social program in a developing country, outside funding often destroys local initiative and sometimes actually corrupts the recipient of these foreign funds. In South Africa, an influential church leader told me that he advises congregations never to depend for more than one-third of their income from outside the country. When offers of foreign funding do occur, he counsels that the donor church be asked to send someone with the money to insure that it is spent for the purpose that it was intended. The problem with foreign money is that it creates dependency, which is precisely the opposite of building self-sufficient indigenous leadership.

While the implication of the foregoing might be to abandon all missions giving, I suspect this would be carrying the point to an extreme. For example, a Kenyan medical doctor that I met in Ethiopia had implemented an innovative public health project in Addis Ababa. A missions organization in the United States, with no trace of colonialism, supplied the majority of her funding for her ever expanding work in Sudan and elsewhere in Africa. Likewise, I encountered a church in Kampala, Uganda, with a remarkable AIDS ministry, inspired, in part, by a white missionary from the United States. He wisely, however, was absent from the church much of the year, raising money for church projects, leaving the leadership of the church to the local population. What was discouraging were the few times that we encountered white missionary pastors in large churches in Africa and Asia that surely would have been better off had local leadership been in charge. In contrast, there was a Canadian missionary in Kenya who clearly had a gift for starting churches; yet, once they were up and running, he transferred the leadership to a local pastor and moved to another location.

---

[8] For example, in 18th century England, as the Methodist movement grew, John Wesley made extensive use of cell groups which he called "class meetings," with laity as leaders.

Finally, globalization and the Internet are affecting the way that churches relate to each other. In an era of more and more independent churches, it is quite easy for relationships to be established between church leaders on different continents that have nothing to do with denominational ties. For example, I encountered pastors in Guatemala, Singapore, and Argentina who are in weekly communication with each other, facilitated by e-mail and inexpensive transcontinental telephone calls. Often these pastors are reading the same books on leadership and organizational theory, and they are swapping ideas on social ministry and worship music. What unites them is a common view of mission, not a denominational structure. As mentioned previously, hundreds of informal networks have been established that function as surrogate denominational structures, with one fundamental difference: They are founded on relationships rather than legal obligations.

Everywhere I have traveled in these countries, I have asked about the health of churches established by mainline U.S. and European denominations. In very few instances have I heard reports of growing Methodist, Presbyterian, or other mainline groups. This even applies to some of the older Pentecostal groups, such as the Assemblies of God, that seem to be saddled with legalistic traditions that worked well for poor people half a century ago but do not currently make sense to middle class and college educated members. Indeed, it appears that denominational affiliation sometimes stultifies growth and innovation. Some of the largest and most innovative churches we visited are independent neo-Pentecostal congregations. In many instances the senior pastor had begun his ministry as part of a denomination until he became fed up with the supervision or slow rate of change and simply struck out on his own.

SOCIAL IMPACT

In the last decade or so, many Pentecostal and charismatic churches around the globe seem to be increasingly catching a vision of addressing the social needs of their communities. Historically, these churches tended to focus on the spiritual needs of potential converts. More recently, however, they have been reading their Bibles through a different lens. Renacer Church in Sao Paulo, for example, sends out

KENYA: Nairobi Chapel clinic

many buses every night, staffed with volunteers, to serve homeless people living under highway bridges and in skid row locations. In each bus is a huge pot containing many gallons of soup, along with fresh water, blankets, and whatever else can be collected and distributed. When the bus arrives on location, the volunteers distribute food and strike up conversations with the recipients, but there is no preaching and no expectation of reciprocation. They are there to serve people because that is what Jesus did, healing the sick and feeding the multitudes.

In Uganda, a Pentecostal church in the capital city of Kampala is responding to the devastating impact of the AIDS crisis on that country. Honoring the cultural custom of the extended family taking in orphans whose parents have died, this church acknowledges that many families are so overburdened with the children of relatives that they can no longer cope. Hence, the church is building villages with housing that can accommodate a single mother and eight children. While several of these children may be the mother's own, the rest are adopted. The church supplies the food for each village, but individual families cook their own meals. Since there are no men in these households, the church—which numbers about 10,000—has established a program called "Father's Heart," where men volunteer to be surrogate fathers to the children.

In nearby Kenya, a Pentecostal church has established a residential vocational school for street children, which is a growing problem because of the AIDS pandemic. They purchased a plot of 50 acres and on this land built dormitories, a woodshop, mechanics workshop, sewing room, library, and meeting hall with dining facilities. A social worker identifies hardcore street children who she thinks have a chance for success—meaning they haven't sniffed too much glue or become too hooked on drugs. After appropriate arrangements with the government, she brings these children to the vocational school where they live until they turn 18 years of age and have become certified with an employable skill.

The list of social programs that we studied is extensive, ranging from "mercy ministries" of providing food and shelter, to community organizing that is addressing structural issues of poverty and justice. What is equally important also is that many converts seem to be experiencing upward social mobility. Why? Because they quit gambling, drinking, and womanizing, and the *indirect* consequence is that they have surplus capital that they can invest into their personal business or their children's education, thus giving them a competitive advantage over their neighbors. These Pentecostal and charismatic churches in the developing world are sometimes ahead of their counterparts in the United States in terms of responding to the social implications of the Christian gospel. A Latino Assemblies of God pastor in Orange County, California, recently told me that he is learning from new immigrants in his church who are coming from Central America. They have a tradition of social ministry that is more developed than the California-based church that is receiving them.

One can speculate about why U.S. Pentecostals sometimes lag behind their sister churches in the developing world. In part it may be a result of the extensive network of public social services available to needy people in the U.S. Such a safety net is not available in the developing world. Hence Christians are expressing their commitment to biblical values by feeding the hungry, clothing the naked, visiting those in prison, and working for social justice.

The contrasting lack of attention to social ministries among North American Pentecostal congregations may also result from their preoccupation with personal sexual "sins"—for example, abortion and homosex-

uality. As a result they have failed to acknowledge the concerns that other Christians have about social justice, poverty, and those who experience disenfranchisement in society. In fact, many North American Pentecostals seem to have bought so thoroughly into capitalist individualism—possibly as a function of their emphasis on individual salvation and personal sanctification—that they have often forfeited any structural critique that runs counter to conservative political ideologies.

Obviously there are exceptions to these generalizations. Some North American Pentecostal congregations are deeply committed to serving the poor and marginalized in the area around them. Also many African American Pentecostal churches in the United States never fell victim to the trap of spiritualizing all social problems. And, very recently, there are Pentecostal Latino churches that seem to be discovering the social implications of the gospel.

Since this topic is the focus of a forthcoming book that Ted Yamamori and I are co-authoring—*Pentecostalism and Social Transformation: A Global Analysis*[9]—I will not elaborate further except to state that the mainline churches no longer have a corner on the social gospel. If anything, because of funding problems, many mainline churches seem to be focused more on survival than on creating innovative new forms of social ministry. Instead, the important headline is that many Pentecostal churches, especially in the developing world, are merging their commitment to spirituality with an agenda on social transformation that is creating innovative models of Christian social service and community organizing.

A FEW FURTHER ELABORATIONS

In concluding these reflections, it undoubtedly is appropriate to define finally what I believe to be the central task of Christian leadership. My simple answer is that *leadership within the Christian community involves, at its heart, helping individuals identify their callings as they commit themselves on a daily basis to discern what the Spirit of God is doing in the world*—a task that I acknowledge is easier described than done. Christian leadership differs from secular leadership because of the moral and spiritual assump-

---

[9] Forthcoming in 2004 from the University of California Press.

tions implied by what it means to be called to be a fol-lower of Jesus Christ. Thus, corporate standards of success, so often held up in leadership literature, are inappropriate for Christian leaders, whether in North American congregations or those that we studied in the Two-Thirds World. Building ever bigger church structures and having increasing numbers of members are not criteria central to Christian discipleship. But teaching people to love God and to love others as much as they love themselves *are* essential bench-marks for Christian leaders. Likewise, leadership involves helping members understand how specific biblical mandates related to ministering to the poor and needy define the agenda of every follower of Christ. In short, the role of the leader is to help peo-ple within the body of Christ to discern their gifts and discover how God is calling them to live as Christian disciples at this moment in time.

If the church is going to be a vital place for transform-ing people's lives, then attention must be given to reex-amining the means of training the next generation of leaders. As has been noted, many leaders of churches in the developing world, as well as leaders of new par-adigm churches in the United States, have refused to adopt the classical model of seminary education. Also, when they need to add to their pastoral staff, they often ignore looking for credentialed pastors from out-side their congregation. Instead they prefer to train up leaders from within their congregation and deploy them for full-time service, once they have demonstrat-ed their calling and gift for leadership.

The reason for hiring from within the congregation is that these new leaders understand the "DNA," so to speak, of the institution, and they have already aligned themselves with that congregation's vision.[10] In contrast, the pattern prominent in most mainline denominations is for pastors to come from outside the congregation, from a pool of seminary-trained pas-tors available to be called or appointed to serve the variety of congregations in the denomination or in other church ministries. Both patterns have strengths and liabilities. New paradigm leadership training has the merit of increasing the likelihood that the leader's vision will be tied to that of the congregation from

which he or she has come—the congregation that the leader has helped to establish or in which his or her vision has been nurtured.

At the same time, such in-house training may truncate the leader's vision of the church, depriving the leader of a broader understanding of the church's traditions and practices, and leaving him or her at the mercy of the lat-est fads in church growth or worship styles, for example. The traditional pattern of theological education, in con-trast, has the merit of giving leaders a vision of the church much broader than that of a single congrega-tion. While it may make it more difficult and take longer for the leader to learn a particular congregation's DNA, that is a price that may be worth paying.

Another way of describing these differences is that new paradigm leadership is based on relationships in the congregation, not functional positionality within a denomination's career structure. Such relationships are

THAILAND: Hope of Bangkok Home for Girls

---

[10] It is probably also true that this pattern of leadership development strengthens the control of the founding pastor over new staff members and the pastors of new congregations planted by the "mother" church. Such control has been evident in new paradigm church movements such as the Vineyard Christian Fellowship and Calvary Chapel that I described in *Reinventing American Protestantism.*

built through years of development. They are not easily transferred to another congregation, unless that congregation is a direct offspring of the mother church and bears its DNA. Hence, when leadership migration does occur, it is typically in the process of planting a new church. As I explained previously, one strategy for starting a new church is to "give away" a senior leader, along with some of the church's key lay leaders, in order to birth a new church on the geographical periphery of the mother church's location. Or, in some instances, the new leader and a group of members may be encouraged physically to move their residence and take new jobs in an entirely new location.

The net effect of this process is that leadership vacancies are created in the mother church. Rather than viewing this as a problem, however, these vacancies are deemed to be an opportunity for new leaders to be developed. Consequently, far from being a static organizational model in which people get entrenched in ego-centered roles of leadership, the model understands the church to be like an organism that is constantly evolving. By creating leadership voids within a congregation, it enables new people to discover their gifts, and in this process their commitment is enhanced to the church, to God, and to the Christian mission is enhanced.

The criterion does not seem to be the list of degrees behind one's name or the size of one's monthly paycheck. More important is the attitude of one's heart.

One of the major problems of a growing church is to create leadership roles for new members. The cell group structure addresses this problem in part, because it radically decentralizes leadership. If, however, the church is not structured around cell groups, then it is important to create other opportunities for leadership by developing new ministries or, alternatively, creating leadership vacancies by establishing new churches in which people can serve. Although stable visionary leadership at the helm of an organization is positive, organizations that become static often lose their creativity, which is the reason that corporations sometimes spin off new companies as a way of promoting innovation. Many churches that have selected vitality and influence and not sheer size as their primary goal are practicing a similar strategy by spinning off new congregations.

If leaders are not being trained in seminaries, what is the source of new leadership? One answer to this question was succinctly stated by Chuck Smith, the founder of the Calvary Chapel network, who said, "God does not call those who are qualified, but qualifies those who are called." Indeed, I have often been surprised by who is in leadership positions in some of these vital congregations, whether they are located in the United States or abroad. The criterion does not seem to be the list of degrees behind one's name or the size of one's monthly paycheck. More important is the attitude of one's heart. The questions guiding the selection of leaders in these new paradigm congregations have very little to do with formal credentials. They include the following: Does the individual have a passionate commitment to God? Does he or she have a vision for transforming people and the world around them? Does the person manifest a Spirit-filled life? If these qualities are in place, then God will give them the skills to carry out the task to which they have been called, regardless of formal training. After all, they say, Jesus used a group of fisherman to establish his kingdom.

Does such a heroic philosophy preclude the role of more formal pastoral training? Obviously new paradigm churches are not inattentive to training their leaders, but as I noted, they often do this by creating "equipping" programs in-house rather than sending people away to a seminary for training. The models vary tremendously. Courses are often scheduled so that working people can attend. Also, while there are lectures and assigned texts, there is a strong emphasis on mentored relationships, with people learning through the act of doing ministry under the supervision of a mentor. Teachers and mentors are not necessarily credentialed individuals themselves; although, they typically have a great deal of knowledge and practical experience about their subject area. At the end of the course, certificates for completion may be distributed, but the emphasis is on job readiness, not on accumulating degrees. In fact, while ordination is necessary in order for individuals to perform various clerical functions, there is often very little ceremony attached to conferring certification on an individual. The prior and more fundamental test is whether the community believes that God has called this individual for service.

THAILAND: Bangkok Baby Home

In describing this alternative pattern of Christian leadership, training, and ecclesiastical organization, I do not want to ignore some of the potential problems associated with it. For one thing, decentralized leadership, as practiced in these new paradigm congregations, can be messy. This is often the case when one moves from authoritarian governance, where a central authority controls all that happens, to the contrasting practice of giving power to the people to develop their own leadership opportunities within the congregation. Most of us learn by making mistakes, and senior church leaders have to give people the space for this learning process to occur while, at the same time making certain that nothing too bizarre happens that could damage the body of Christ or individuals within it. It is for that reason that decentralized authority structures must still have built-in systems of checks and balances. Some years ago, for example, the Vineyard Christian Fellowship was faced with what came to be called the "Toronto Blessing," with people at a Vineyard congregation in Toronto engaging in "Holy Laughter" and manifesting various barnyard animal sounds. After much deliberation, the late John Wimber, the Vineyard Fellowship's founder and head, decided to "disfellowship" the Toronto congregation because he could find no biblical warrant for what was occurring.

Second, there are tendencies towards biblical literalism and anti-intellectualism in these churches and their pat-tern of training leaders—tendencies that seminary education often counteracts in important ways. I have no doubt that there needs to be a balance between openness to the Spirit of God and knowing how Christians through the ages have thought and written about God and God's work in the world. New paradigm leaders—sometimes with justification—accuse seminaries of essentially reducing God and God's purposes to conceptual abstractions. But their criticism is more often a caricature. It is important that even the most successful pastor of a growing, socially conscious church have some historical perspective on how his or her congregation relates to the last 2,000 years of Christian history. Simply claiming the authority of scripture and attempting to replicate the first century church is not enough. Church leaders need to know how the church has struggled to be faithful (or failed to do so) through the centuries. They need to know something about battles that have been fought over theological doctrines. And they need also to develop the capacity to "read" and critique their culture through the lenses of Christian theology and ethics, lenses that formal theological education often provides. Thus, unless Christian leaders want to narrow their appeal to those who resist any form of intellectual concern, then it is important that they understand the evolution of the church, the history of doctrine, and gain the capacity for ethical and theological reflection—among the various contributions of theological education.

Moreover, it is important that such leaders gain the capacity for *self*-criticism that the resources of Christian teaching and experience offer. Such resources are also the fruit in part of formal theological education where one is regularly challenged to engage in self-reflection and critique. These are virtues that I have found to be sometimes lacking in self-trained leaders of new paradigm churches who presume to know the Spirit's leading without any attempt to test whether the leading is from God or not.

At the same time, however, I am convinced that seminaries need dramatic restructuring—especially if they are to be relevant within the developing world but also in the North American context. If that were not the case, then some of the most vital churches of the 21st century would not be setting up alternative training programs. Indeed, the kind of on-the-job mentoring done in these churches may provide important clues to ways that seminary education might be restructured to train leaders—but not, I believe, by setting formal classroom learning over against on-the-job learning. Rather I believe that what is needed are innovative ways of melding the two into a synergy, so that new leaders gain the intellectual grounding in scripture, church history, doctrine, and cultural analysis that provide them with the "why" of pastoral leadership *and* have the opportunity for on-the job development of leadership skills and techniques that give them the "how." At the same time, neither of these contexts will be adequate if they fail to form students spiritually, forming them with the habits of prayer, reflection, and meditation that characterize the vital leaders that I described earlier in this essay. Such formation is essential if they are to lead Spirit-filled churches.

Third, there is the poignant question of whether old ecclesial structures can or even should be reformed, or whether it is better to invent new ones from the ground up. Quite frankly, this question can only be answered by individuals who are listening to the call of God on their own lives, for I assume that the body of Christ will always be multiform and not uniform. The history of the Christian church is a tug-of-war (or something even more violent) between what Ernst Troeltsch identified as the church, sect, and mystic types. Although this typology is too constraining for what I have been observing, the point is still valid that the church-type of social organization is, by definition, bureaucratic and routinized, while the sect is reformist, populist, and filled with visions of spiritual purity. The mystic, in contrast, has typically abandoned what he or she views as the corruption of organized religion to pursue God in individualistic and privatized ways.

Although there is room for all three expressions of discipleship within the Christian church, my personal fascination is clearly with the reformist movements, which, I believe, need not always exhibit sectarian characteristics of exclusivity and isolation from secular encounters. In fact, some of the best examples of reform-oriented churches are congregations, some of them large, which are confronting social issues and engaging and collaborating with secular institutions rather than withdrawing in lonely isolation. Furthermore, many of these reformist congregations are welcoming diverse types of people into their ranks, encouraging them to grow in their faith and discern and act on God's call for their lives.

As leaders listen to the call of God's Spirit, it is undoubtedly prudent for them to pay a great deal of attention to their constituency. I doubt that aging congregations are going to be up for some of the radical changes that I have described. Such measures would probably be divisive—the so-called "worship wars" over the introduction of contemporary forms and music are an example. At the same time, denominations and their member congregations should unquestionably think about ways of creating new organizational forms and practices—some of them drawn from the church's tradition—that will connect with a younger generation who typically feel alienated from the standard format for "doing church." Alternatively, some Christians will work outside of the existing denominational structures, as is the case of many independent congregations and parachurch organizations. I do not doubt that this is healthy. Reform oftentimes is stimulated through competition, with non-functional organizations and practices failing to survive as new forms and practices come into being. But these new forms and practices, however innovative, will also need regularly to be renewed, else they too will ossify and die.

VENEZUELA: Don Miller and friend, Caracas

SOME IMMODEST PROPOSALS

The odyssey that I have described in the preceding pages has convinced me that we, as North American Christians, must surrender any lingering assumptions that we may have about our superior status as members of the body of Christ. Along with this admission should come a reexamination of the legacy of western colonialism which was often given expression in Christian missions. Western Christians are but a single candle bearing witness to the truth that God has elected to share with us. In all humbleness we should seek ways to partner with and learn from other Christian communities around the world. And in these attempts we should put our checkbooks in our pockets, because dangling money in front of churches in the developing world has the potential of perpetuating colonial control or, even worse, invite corruption. Thus I offer several "immodest" proposals.

My first proposal is that every church in the United States should create a relationship with a church in the developing world. The first year or two should be spent with members and leaders visiting each other, sharing ideas on worship and community outreach, but, more importantly, breaking bread together and getting to know each other's cultures, needs, and aspirations. These relationships need not be within denominational boundaries. For example, would it not be wonderful for an Episcopal or a Presbyterian congregation in Los Angeles to step outside its comfort zone and form a relationship with a Pentecostal church in Ghana? If we are to understand globalization, then we need to move beyond the polarized debates that we read about in the press, and instead form long-lasting relationships with people around the world. These relationships must be characterized by mutuality, not missionary zeal or paternalism. We in the West clearly have something to learn about spirituality from churches in the developing world, along with their innovative approaches to addressing intractable problems related to poverty and health. In turn, people in the West have a longstanding understanding of the inner workings of capitalism and global markets that can be extremely useful to people in the developing world. However, as I have emphasized, direct aid to churches in the Two-Thirds World from those in the West may be a mistake—at least initially—because it is important not to commercialize relationships that have barely gotten off the ground.

My second recommendation has to do with restructuring seminaries. I believe there would be great value in holding a series of consultations in which seminary presidents and deans would meet with leaders of fast-growing new paradigm churches around the world in order to start a dialogue about the needs associated with creating strong Christian leaders. Initially, discussion of agendas related to institutional maintenance should be bracketed, including investment in buildings, high status faculty, library systems, and so forth. Rather, the focus should be on the needs of rapidly expanding churches, the need for a contextual understanding of the Christian tradition, and whatever else participants want to put on the table. There would be no expectation that the goal of the consultation would be the birth a new model of Christian leadership development. Instead, the aim would be open exchange of ideas.

These consultations should be held outside of North America, preferably in different locations in the developing world. Extensive pre-planning would be done by a small group of potential participants, ensuring that the agenda and structure of the consultation are mutually owned and embraced by all. An independent moderator would be selected who does not have vested interests. And ample time would be allotted for participants to socialize informally.

Three or four months after the first consultation, working papers would be circulated that would describe new models of theological education and leadership training. A second round of consultations would then be held, with representatives of foundations and board members invited to listen in on the conversations. Ideally, this consultation, as well as the first round of meetings, would include representatives from independent churches as well as non-traditional denominations, since creating new models that simply conform to the old structures would be a serious mistake.

At the end of these consultations, there would be redrafting, re-visioning, and re-imagining. Hopefully the Spirit of God would take control of the process, and Christians of all stripes and backgrounds would be led to build on the relationships that had been developed. Being a realist, I don't think anything too revolutionary would emerge, but on the other hand the implementation of such a process might help to further the work of the Kingdom, shattering some of the polarization, anger, and frustration that currently reside between many established seminaries and their potential constituents.

VENEZUELA: Church youth, Caracas

My third recommendation has to do with the various means by which Christians around the world are attempting to manifest God's love in the face of global poverty, the AIDS pandemic, and a hundred other needs associated with the human inclination toward greed and violence. Personally, I feel very privileged to have had the opportunity to travel extensively, witnessing many different efforts by Christians around the world to be God's agents of healing, reconciliation, and justice. In this process, I have been struck by how creative and entrepreneurial Christians in the developing world are in addressing intractable social problems, but, unfortunately, many of these programs exist in isolation.

Consequently, I believe that there is a great need to share the wealth—the wealth of ideas, the wealth of vision—because we in the West can learn from what our brothers and sisters are doing, and we can partner with them in expanding these programs. The challenge, of course, is how this undertaking can be accomplished, and there is no easy answer.

I do, however, have several suggestions. First, if we were to develop thousands of church-to-church partnerships between congregations in the West with worshipping communities in the developing world, then we would become more aware of these Spirit-filled, faith-based social ministries. Secondly, we need to help build the capacity of research centers in the developing world that can gather these stories and be a hub for information exchange. And, thirdly, we need to create a substantial Internet database of these promising practices that will be constantly updated.[11] Clearly, foundation assistance would be necessary to help launch these three proposals, but one should not forget the important role that local congregations can play, including many of the affluent new paradigm churches.

In conclusion, I will simply restate the premise of my reflections and these several proposals. I believe that the locus of the Christian church has changed poles. It is no longer in the West or the Northern Hemisphere. Therefore, a paradigm shift in our thinking is in order that reflects this changed locus of the church's constituencies. I suggest that it begin by Christians in North America entering a steep, experiential learning curve. Now is a good time to change the family vacation travel itinerary in order to visit a church south of the equator. And it is also a good time to augment the travel budget of the senior members of your church's clergy. September 11, 2001, was a wakeup call to our nation. Churches have an obligation to better understand our global context, and there is no finer way to do this than at the human level, forging partnerships of collaborative learning.

---

[11] Internet access is increasingly available in all parts of the developing world, and there is no more economical way to disseminate this information than through this electronic medium.

YET ONE MORE FACE

A Response by Daniel Aleshire
Executive Director, Association of Theological Schools in the United States and Canada

Donald Miller takes his readers on a brief and inviting tour of congregations that he has studied in the developing world, including Kenya, Brazil, Ethiopia; and supplements the findings of his research with the significant data that David Barrett and his associates have assembled on the religious geography of the world. The growth of Christianity has shifted from the West and North to the East and South. Asia, Africa, and South America are centers of extraordinary growth in the Christian religion, and they are redefining the center of gravity of Christianity. These new and rapidly growing Christian movements are more likely to be Evangelical, especially Pentecostal, or Roman Catholic than historic U.S. mainline Protestants, and whatever their denomination, they are characterized by more singing, congregational warmth, and spiritual vitality than their North American fraternal communions. The ministry of large congregations in developing countries focuses on physical well-being and community development needs as well as spiritual transformation and personal piety.

In the Christian communities he studied, leadership typically grows from within large congregations, and reflects their ethos, vision of faith, and patterns of ministry. While pastors may be university educated, they are not likely to be seminary graduates. Rather, they have been trained by other pastors, in the context of congregational work and worship, in the ministerial style and spirit of the teaching congregation. Miller notes that these leaders are not "personality" focused, but are committed to developing lay leaders who often share highly visible leadership with pastors. These pastors are deeply committed to the Christian faith; they are, deeply and devotedly, Christian believers. These congregations eagerly plant new churches and their strategy involves sending both members and leaders from large congregations to new congregational starts.

"Leadership within the Christian community," in his analysis, "involves helping individuals identify their callings and commit themselves on a daily basis to discern what the Spirit of God is doing in the world." And, on the basis of this definition and the effectiveness of leadership that Miller has observed in congregations in developing nations, he argues that it is necessary to reexamine the means of training the next generation of leaders, and, with due respect for what Western-style seminaries have contributed to the education of leaders in North America, he is convinced that seminaries need "dramatic restructuring."

I have not visited the congregations that Professor Miller describes, but from everything I know about Christianity as it is manifesting itself in this new century, Miller is right. The center of gravity of the Christian faith has shifted, and the shift has not just been the movement of Western European and North American Christianity to other parts of the world. The shift also entails the invention of new patterns of worship, new styles of congregational life and work, and different approaches to leadership education. These descriptions correspond to what I have read and everything that I have heard in conversations at North American seminaries, which are the schools I have studied and where I spend most of my time. Miller writes as a social science researcher who is able to take delight in the integrity of emergent Christianity in developing countries. His descriptions about these new Christian movements evoke only agreement and appreciation from me. I found myself, however, less in agreement with the some of the implications he has drawn from these movements for North American Protestantism and theological education. I want to respond in two general ways: the first concerns the phenomena of emerging Christian communities; and the second concerns the implications for the education of Christian leaders.

1. DEVELOPING CHRISTIANITY

The current patterns of growth and change that Miller describes are not new to the Christian project; they have been a part of the development of Christianity at other times and in other places. In the United States, for example. I think that very similar descriptions could have been made a century or century and a half ago as Methodist circuit riders and Baptist preachers took a more lively and revivalistic Protestantism to frontier towns and villages. England and Europe had seen little of the kind of Christianity that was emerging on the American frontier. It grew fast, with new churches starting everywhere a revival had broken out, most of them teeming with expressionistic versions of Christian worship that would have impressed a 19th century European soci-ologist, had there been one. As Christianity moved into the frontier, the education of leaders changed, as well. Methodists and Baptists were not likely to have attended college or seminary, but would have read with another pastor, and been educated on the job. Had they graduated from Harvard, Yale, Andover, or Newton in early 19th century, they likely would have found their theological education inadequate for the pastoral leadership that was needed in the Kentucky mountains or along the Mississippi delta. Christianity took on still new forms as Southern whites shared it with their slaves, who took their masters' religion and transformed its practices and passions into expressions that had not been seen before. The "new" Christian movement that was described in this essay is

similar to "new" Christian movements that have flourished in other places, in differ-ent cultures, at different times. I think that the essay accurately docu-ments that what has happened in the past is happening again. This new expression is not the new face of Christianity; it is yet one more face, of which there have been many, and of which there will be many more.

This new expression is not the new face of Christianity; it is yet one more face, of which there have been many, and of which there will be many more.

Christianity has a way of re-inventing itself as a movement, and I see these re-inventions as works of the Spirit that inevitably lead to social organizational structures. These structures establish and institution-alize these new expressions, including ordering a style of ministry and education that fits an institutionalized religious community. For example, as 19th century American denominations formed and grew, denomi-national colleges and seminaries were founded for the training of ministers. These schools were the result of new Christian commitments and passions, and many of the mainline seminaries that Miller wants to reform were founded in the 19th century as the conse-quence of optimistic, growing expressions of faith. A similar pattern has characterized events in the 20th century. An examination of the seminaries that have been founded since World War II demonstrates that the vast majority are Evangelical, including four

Pentecostal schools. These newer seminaries reflect the passions and commitments of new or reformist Christian movements in the United States, which have been primarily Evangelical.

This essay seems to want to contrast new Christian movements in developing countries with mainline Protestantism in North America. That is fine, and mainline Protestants have much to learn. However, it creates two problems. First, when a new religious movement in a different culture is compared to some-thing almost two centuries old in another culture, it is difficult to determine how much of the difference is a function of age, how much is a function of culture, and how much is a function of a work of the Spirit. If we were to turn the clock back 200 years, would we argue that English Protestants would have been better to have adopted the styles of Christianity that were emerging on the American frontier or in slave church-es? Perhaps it would have been, but cultural and social contexts were sufficiently different that adoption of these new practices would have been difficult. Second, to the extent that these developments are a "work of the Spirit," it is difficult to imagine how they can be duplicated apart from a similar providential initiative. While I celebrate the emergence of new Christian movements, and think that they should be carefully studied and celebrated by North American Christians, I am not sure how instructive they are for organized Christianity in North America, with its dif-ferent history, different culture, and itself the heir of another powerful, emergent religious sentiment. American mainline Protestantism has major problems, is in a 30 year decline, and has lost the social status that it once had. Reform is the order of the day. I'm just not sure that the experiences of emergent Christian communities are the key to that reform.

2. EDUCATING PASTORAL LEADERS

Professor Miller clearly has a reformist agenda with regard to North American theological edu-cation. What should be done with the seminar-ies that grew up in North America as Christianity was inventing new expressions and institutionalizing new patterns of social organization? Education, particular-ly professional education, is very culturally bounded. American legal education, for example, would not travel well to Kenya or Ethiopia. The practice of law, not to mention the legal systems themselves, are too different for the same educational system to work well in North America and these developing countries. I think the same is true for theological education. That US-style seminaries were ever established in these countries was probably a mistake. They may have worked as long as national churches were missionary extensions of North American churches, but as national churches mature, with their own cultural and theological integrity, North American seminary structures will not work. It is no surprise that pastors in the congregations that Miller studied did not attend seminaries. However, it would be a mistake to assume that because something does not work well in the developing world it should be dramatically reformed in North America.

Theological education on this continent reflects the dominant educational system in the culture, and as new religious movements emerge in this country, new seminaries are formed. These new schools generally follow the graduate, professional school model, I think, because of its widespread cultural acceptance. They are founded to provide education for leaders in communities that follow a new or reformed religious vision, and to undertake the intellectual labor that the vision will, over time, require. Not only are new seminaries formed, seminaries, new and old, reform educational practices. Many ATS schools have developed extension programs, adopted distance education programs, and in other ways, have sought to get theological education to practicing ministers rather than to educate candidates who have little or no ministerial experience.

Although Professor Miller attempts to balance his criticism of North American theological education with appreciation for its strengths, he does not seem to be fully aware of the diversity that presently exists or of efforts being made to respond to a number of the criticisms he makes. In the United States, Evangelical Protestant schools are becoming the dominant presence in theological education. Approximately 49 percent of the students in ATS schools in 2001 were enrolled in schools that would identify themselves, in one way or another, as Evangelical. I wish that he were more acquainted with schools like the Assemblies of God Theological Seminary, or Church of God Theological Seminary, or Oral Roberts School of Theology, or Bethel Theological Seminary, or Asbury Theological

Seminary, or the Seventh-day Adventist Theological Seminary, or Southwestern Baptist Theological Seminary, or Columbia Biblical Seminary, or even the School or World Mission at his Pasadena neighbor, Fuller Theological Seminary. These schools are intensely aware of the accuracy of the description that this essay provides, and as schools, are being transformed by the changing character of Christianity in other parts of the world.

I also know that these schools are being called upon to provide theological education in the very parts of the world that this essay describes. Apparently, even in these areas, there is a perceived need for the kind of education that seminaries provide. I think that U.S. seminaries are providing this education at the request of local Christians in these developing countries because there are educational needs these schools can meet. These needs are not so much about pastoral practice as they are about understanding the history of the church, the interpretation of its scripture, the skills that can increase effectiveness in new cultural settings, and teaching the persons who will be the teachers.

But what about the mainline Protestant schools? Have they become irrelevant to the theological education of pastors in mainline Protestant settings? These schools have considerable work to do, because their founding denominations are changing, and it appears to me that they are doing it. They are thinking aggressively about how to contribute more effectively to the education of alternatively credentialed clergy a growing phenomenon in mainline congregations. They are becoming much more informed about the education of students that are diverse in every way, including denominational background. They are providing education for an increasing number of racial/ethnic students, and have demonstrated a commitment to attend to the needs of racial/ethnic communities, which are clearly the centers of new vitality in American Christianity. As mainline denominations have retrenched in the past several decades, and their colleges, hospitals, and child welfare agencies have distanced themselves from their founding denominations, the seminaries have become some of the last institutions the denominations still have, and that has meant that the seminaries have assumed roles and provided programs that denominational offices would have provided in another era. A seminary exists in a religious community for a variety of reasons, one of which is the education of pastors and other leaders.

There is still more work to do. About 40 percent of the 244 ATS member schools participate in a survey of graduates each year. More than 4,000 graduates in the 2001-02 academic year completed the survey, and on a five point Likert scale, they rated relatively their satisfaction in progress in 15 skill areas related to future work. They are satisfied, for the most part (nine of the skills were rated in 4+ range, and six in the 3.6+ range). Of these 15 areas, however, graduates rated satisfaction with progress in their skill related to "ability to administer a parish" least positively. This is not a mainline issue, it is a theological school issue, and it confirms some of the supposition that Miller brings to his essay. Theological schools are better at education in the biblical, historical, and theological disciplines than they are the pastoral arts. They need to become better at the kind of clinical education that enhances ministerial and priestly practice.

Theological schools–even mainline Protestant ones—are adaptive social organizations. They change as the religious constituencies they serve change. Because schools are organizationally conservative, whatever their theology may be, changes are typically slow. Many North American schools, however, have already changed in such substantive ways that it is hard for an accrediting agency like ATS to keep up with them. I worry that some schools might outlive the religious enthusiasms that founded them, but I am convinced they will find communities to serve and needed forms of education to provide.

Christianity, as had been true in the past, is changing, and as it changes, the patterns of education that will be needed for religious leaders will change. As these patterns change, old schools will adapt to new patterns of education and other, new schools will be founded to embody them.

THAILAND: Bangkok worship service

MEASURING SUCCESS, DEVELOPING LEADERS

A Response by Chad Hall, Team Leader, Innovative Church Team, Baptist State Convention of N.C.
Lead Pastor, Connection Church, Hickory, N.C.

In *Emergent Patterns*, Don Miller examines and translates Third-World Christianity for a Western mainline audience and provides helpful beginning points for coming to terms with what is happening on these geographically and practically distant fronts. Miller's report complements other recent explorations of Christianity's explosive growth in the Latin, Asian, and African parts of the world (including articles in *Newsweek* and *The Atlantic Monthly*) and makes an important contribution to the conversation. His report helps make the Christianity of the developing world both accessible and inspirationally prescriptive for Christians in the United States.

In my opinion, the hope for implementing lessons from the developing world rests with the innovators and early adapters within the American church leadership population. Miller hints at one segment of this potentially receptive population when he talks about the emerging generation of leaders in American churches. This group of new generation leaders, who Robert Webber refers to as "Younger Evangelicals," seem to carry a discontent with typical American Christianity that opens them to findings such as Miller's. These leaders are both young and old and they are in the minority of leaders in Western Christianity. It is within such groups that new models of leadership will most likely take root.

American church leaders who seek to implement lessons learned from Third-World churches should find many lessons that will apply to the American context. One of the greatest lessons for us is a focused cognizance of God's activity in contexts that are neither Western, Modern, nor mainline. For us to see and experience (be it through firsthand encounters or through reports such as Miller's) God's movement in these contexts offers an encounter that is certain to impact both our understanding and our practice of Christianity in many ways. Though the implications are manifold, I believe the implications will revolve around two foci – how we measure success and how we develop leaders.

CHANGING OUR CATEGORIES FOR MEASURING SUCCESS

Churches in the developing world are pursuing success in categories that differ from those used by most American congregations. It seems that these developing world believers are focused on proclaiming the gospel so that spiritual, emotional, and physical healing can occur through persons' supernatural encounters with God. Much of what has happened in and through these churches has gone unnoticed by Westerners not because we were incognizant, but because these churches have succeeded in categories that we do not evaluate.

Churches in the developing world help us to reconsider our ministry success in terms of social impact and personal spiritual transformation by bringing a balanced approach to these two important factors. American churches often find themselves out of kilter by exaggerating the importance of one of these factors over the other. Pentecostal and evangelical congregations tend to stress personal transformation to the neglect of social impact, while mainline and liberal churches go to the opposite extreme. As we witness congregations in the developing world find a balance of these Gospel expressions, we can better define success in our own contexts according to both/and categories rather that either/or dichotomies.

The success of churches in the developing world can also shift us away from an overemphasis on financial success. In my work with new churches planted in the Southeastern U.S., a recurring theme is the need for more money. As a leader of a new church, I also find myself measuring our congregation's success by our bank account, offering receipts, and financial gifts from partnering churches. The emphasis on money certainly is not unique to new churches. Most likely, a congregation's interest in dollars rests dually on the need for staff salaries and the fact that many Americans gauge our personal well being according to financial standards. But the success of very poor people in experiencing the good news of God's love forces us to rethink the central role of money in our church lives. More money will not necessarily result in more ministry, more life change, or more spiritual renewal. Like some of the people described in Acts, we may need to learn that God's healing, resurrecting, and forgiving Spirit cannot be bought.

Another current category for measuring success is acclaim from other American church leaders. From Miller's report and others like it, we cannot deny that God is at work among and through the churches in the developing world. Not only is God at work in these churches, but also the level of divine impact in these areas is stunning. And this success has largely gone unnoticed by the majority of American churches. It seems that every American congregation with a few thousand members warrants the title "teaching congregation." The leaders of these churches write books, speak at seminars, and are held in high regard by their peers. I am not saying that the attention and commendations are unwarranted, but they should not be confused for success or even as a sign of success. The stealth success of churches in the developing world forces us to reconsider whether praise from our peers has anything to do with Gospel success.

Finally, the churches of the emerging world can aid us in rethinking the limits of theological orthodoxy as a measure of success. In a post-Christendom and postmodern context, theological minimalism may be the grandest of theological developments. Emerging world churches appear to be more passionate about expressing God's love, power, and purpose than about fully understanding God or these expressions. Popular American writers and thinkers such as Leonard Sweet, Tom Bandy, and Brian McLaren are already ushering in a minimalist approach among mainline and evangelical church leaders. They are doing so in an effort to help us deal with a context in which our ability to minister effectively as Christ's ambassadors rests more on our participation in a unique community (with a few important beliefs) than on nuanced belief branding that serves to distinguish various tribes within the larger family of faith. With the added voices of developing world churches, American church leaders may find that ever-expanding systematic theologies are unnecessary baggage for a context in which it is better to travel light.

> *I believe that seminaries will lose status as the centerpieces for preparing men and women to be successful congregational leaders.*

CHANGING HOW WE DEVELOP LEADERS

From *Emergent Patterns*, it appears that the success of churches in the developing world has much to do with their unique approaches to leadership. Should these leadership practices gain currency among American believers, the implications are manifold – especially for theological training. Based on the churches described by Miller, we will be well-served to consider whether to supplement, discard, or reinforce our various leadership development experiences. Training that is scholastic, short-term, and static pales in comparison to the leadership development models described by Miller. An entire report could be written on how these developing world churches and their methods for raising up leaders can impact American seminaries. To put it briefly, the impact is at least threefold.

First, I believe that seminaries will lose status as the centerpieces for preparing men and women to be successful congregational leaders. I do not think I am overstating this implication, and in fact this reality is already being felt. In many evangelical, Pentecostal, and independent churches in America, seminary training is far less important a criterion for becoming a church leader than is proven giftedness and humility. I believe this has much to do with the move toward theological minimalism mentioned earlier. The context for doing ministry in America will more and more resemble that of the developing world in that churches will become more pragmatically focused on expanding the kingdom and less interested in academic discussions about ministry. It is easy to imagine the pendulum swinging too far in the pragmatic direction, but that does not change the pendulum's momentum. As believers continue to put more stock in clergy's demonstrated ability to lead, less weight will be given to academic degrees and formal theological training. The question of "How has God empowered you to lead us to accomplish the mission God has given us?" will replace "Are you trained and well-versed in the distinctions of our particular tradition?" In some contexts, this shift will make seminary training an accessory at best or a liability at worst.

Second, seminary leaders who take Miller's report seriously will strive to help students better integrate academic training and real-world ministry experience so that leadership potential is incubated by the seminary experience. Most seminaries make some attempts at this already. However, these efforts typically result in ministry experiences that are minor supplements to classroom-based curricula. In programs seeking to prepare men and women to be successful church leaders, Church Ministry courses might move from being a discipline within the larger M.Div. curricula to being the framework for the entire program. This shift in focus means that Biblical Studies, Theology, and Church History courses will be judged on how well they actually prepare students to do ministry in a real-world context. Along with curriculum changes, seminaries will want to spend vast amounts of time, energy, and other resources helping students scrutinize their ministry experiences (experiences that will take place concurrently with classes). In addition, new systems for accepting, matriculating, grading, and ordaining students will be needed in order to build a seminary culture focused on fostering leadership growth as opposed to rewarding academic achievement. Already, students know that grade performance in seminary has little correlation with post-seminary leadership success. The schools that acknowledge this disparity and begin to overhaul their approach will succeed in the theological training marketplace of the next century.

Third, seminaries will become involved in learning/training triads. As the developing world churches demonstrate, each leader-in-training has ministry specific needs. Also, because leaders are attracted to leadership roles, young leaders will likely serve a congregation while receiving theological training. For these reasons, schools might consider partnering with students and congregations to design learning experiences that more deeply reflect the unique needs of each student and the congregation she serves. The development of learning/training triads will mean that seminaries have less voice in dictating what a student shall learn. In this sense, the seminary will become the agent to whom a congregation outsources one aspect of a developing leader's training program and each student

will have a unique training experience both in content and in length. This approach will have uncertain implications for degree programs. It may mean that more clergy will seek certificates or issue-specific courses as opposed to completing full-fledged degree programs. Also, if students and congregations have increased input into what happens at the seminary, the seminary will need to have reciprocal input into the training that occurs within the ministry setting. Congregations who train leaders through internships, learning communities, and shadowing experiences will want to invite seminaries into the conversations that determine what these parish-based learning experiences look like.

CONCLUSION

The world that Miller describes is not as far away from mainline America as one might think. Among a growing number of American congregations I have observed many aspects of what Miller describes in his report. These trends are already impacting us, and *Emergent Patterns* serves to help us recognize these trends more easily. Certainly not every characteristic of Christianity in the developing world will replicate itself among American congregations, but as the Church leans more heavily toward the South and East, toward postmodernity, and toward charismatic Christianity, American congregations will be impacted. Perhaps Miller's greatest contribution is that by raising the issues he helps readers decide whether to brace for these shifts, embrace these shifts, or do both.

SOUTH AFRICA: Highway Nursery School

ADAPTABILITY AND PRINCIPLE

A Response by Grant Wacker
Professor of Church History, Duke University Divinity School, Durham, N.C.

Several years ago I received an invitation to give a lecture at one of the oldest and strongest of the American Pentecostal seminaries. Just before I stood to talk, the president asked the students if anyone needed prayer. One middle-aged woman said that she had been diagnosed with cancer. The president asked her to step forward. He looked around the pulpit area for anointing oil. Finding none, he turned to the students and asked if anyone had hair spray. Someone passed a small canister to the front. The president took it, dabbed a bit on the woman's forehead, laid hands on her head, and fervently prayed for her healing. He then turned, smiled, and introduced me as warmly as he might have introduced a long-lost relative.

I open with this scenario because it succinctly illustrates the key point highlighted in Professor Miller's perceptive essay. This point might be summarized as *adaptability in the service of principle*. Both terms are important: adaptability and principle. The former without the latter leaves the ship rudderless and adrift; the latter without the former leaves the vessel stranded on the rocks of obsolescence.

The integration of adaptability and principle reveals itself in numerous ways in the life of developing-world churches, but it stands out with particular clarity in Miller's depiction of new leadership styles and new organizational patterns.

Miller does not systematically sketch the characteristics of new leaders in any one spot but, considered whole, a composite portrait readily emerges. First of all—and surely most important in their own minds—new leaders feel that they have undergone a "radical, life-changing encounter with God." (9) This encounter nurtures the conviction that they are "connected with the deepest truths and realities available to the human species." Given this foundation, it is not surprising to find that they "commune with God; they seek God's presence; they await divine instructions." (12) I suspect that these features taken together—encounter, conviction, and communion—constitute as useful a definition of charisma as one is likely to discover in the whole of sociological and historical literature on religious leaders.

But there is more. New leaders see the world as a theater for the direct action of the divine in history. In this respect their outlook differs from most mainline Christians, especially those in the Protestant tradition. They evince an "expectant spirit, believing that God will enter human history," just as he did in times past. (9) Miller suggests that new leaders' willingness to see the supernatural all around them stems from the encounter with God in their personal lives. I agree, but I would add that it also stems from their attitude toward the Bible. Miller tells us that new leaders are "voracious readers of scripture." This devotional habit rests on the assumption that the Bible offers a transparent lens for viewing the miraculous events of ancient times and, equally important, that the miraculous events described in the Bible serve as a template for the church's life today. These are potent ideas, and they bear potent consequences.

These two traits—charisma and supernaturalism—lead to a third: innovativeness. Indeed, innovativeness may be what outsiders see first. To be sure, new leaders themselves probably would rank it pretty low on any list of their own virtues, and many would not countenance it at all, for they believe that God's Spirit does everything. But viewed from afar, Miller's account leaves little doubt that new leaders are distinguished by their innovativeness or, to use a more worldly term, entrepreneurialism. When the older structures do not work, he tells us, they "strike out on their own." Miller intimates but does not expand on the downside of this trait. When blocked, innovative personalities easily turn into mavericks. The romance of the maverick should not obscure the plain fact that over the centuries institutional and denominational structures have come into existence partly to keep come-outer souls under rein. The Marlboro Man looks better on television than in real life.

Finally, new leaders evince little regard for formal seminary training. It is important to be precise here. They do not disregard advanced education in general—indeed, many are university-trained—but they show little interest in the standard, seminary-based educational ladder. One might add to Miller's analysis that this pattern is common among groups that assume that the requisite gifts and graces of ministry are available to all believers (including, especially, restorationist bodies like the Churches of Christ and the Latter-day Saints, which esteem secular but not theological education). In this respect, as in many others, new leaders differ from other Christian groups

PHILLIPINES: Jesus is Lord Church

One recurrent theme is new organizations' propensity to divide into cell groups. In doing so they provide an intimacy of fellowship often not available in larger and especially larger mainline bodies. Converts hug, embrace, and kiss. They instinctively understand the therapeutic power of human touch. In Miller's words, "There is often a sweetness in the air that can only be felt and not described." (14)

Dividing into cell groups serves additional needs, such as giving potential leaders a chance to test their skills. If they prove wanting, they can pursue other vocational channels sooner rather than later. If they prove gifted, they can take over the guidance of their own cell group. The process is cost-effective, both in the obvious sense that it is cheap to train new leaders this way, and in the not so obvious sense that success on the ground serves as the acid test of readiness.

My own research on early American Pentecostals suggests that dividing into cell groups performs yet another function—one that Miller does not mention. In brief, it allows leaders already comfortably in place to deflect pressure from insurgents. This suggestion is not as cynical as it may seem. Insurgents can do harm as well as good. Most often, perhaps, they do both harm and good at once. The organization, which typically seeks its own preservation, instinctively understands this truth. So rather than simply crushing or excluding insurrectionaries, it tries to gain the benefits of their energies while avoiding their liabilities.

Miller emphasizes the quality of worship in new organizations. Quality, in this case, means frequency, intensity, and effectiveness in promoting both social reform and personal holiness of life. One of the most fruitful products of Miller's research is his concern to explode the myth that new churches in the developing world lack a vision for concrete measures of social reconstruction. It is high time someone said so. Groups like the Salvation Army do not make the index in most accounts of Christian social reform, but they should. For generations such groups have implemented Christ's care for the "least of these" at the grass roots level of daily life. Equally important is the way that new organizations redefine what counts as social reform. Though they may not spend a lot of time agitating for laws that will, say, reconfigure

not so much by inventing fresh trends as by amplifying or sharpening ones already present.

In place of seminary education, new leaders emphasize one-to-one mentoring and discipleship. Miller suggests that this trait reflects both common sense and biblical literalism (this is the way Jesus and Paul did it). I would go a step further and say that it also reflects a thin appreciation of history or, more precisely, a sense that what counts is the immediate past, the example of one's immediate forebears, not those long dead and now irrelevant. This disregard for seminary training and the concomitant regard for direct mentoring is, to adapt the words of historian Roger G. Robins, a kind of plain folk modernism.[10] The norm of theological construction and practice lies in the needs of the present, not the antique past. The strength of this posture is its freshness and vitality; its weakness is its deafness to the wisdom of tradition.

Miller makes clear that new leaders create new organizations, and this insight brings us to the second major aspect of his research on developing-world churches. Several themes replay throughout.

---

[10] Adapted from Roger G. Robins, *Plain Folk Modernist: The Radical Holiness World of A. J. Tomlinson* (New York: Oxford University Press, forthcoming 2003).

labor/industrial relations, they do spend a lot of time building orphanages, providing AIDS relief, and drilling wells in parched regions.

And then there is personal holiness, or what jaded Christians of the West might dismiss as "lifestyle choices." Miller rightly notes that conversion enhances financial standing by prohibiting or at least diminishing the amount of money wasted on tobacco, alcohol, gambling, and partying with one's friends. Miller also notes but does not amplify as fully as he might the revolutionary implications of a single, not double, ethic for men in matters of sexual temptation.[11]

New organizations emerge in Miller's research as decentralized. They eschew central bureaucracies and sending agencies in favor of congregational polity and voluntary missionary efforts. But this pattern is more complex than first appears. For one thing, ordinary believers commonly delegate power to leaders who speak on their behalf.

> *If students already knew what they are supposed to know, they would be the teachers.*

Miller tactfully sidesteps the obvious: such figures can be as autocratic as any up-town bureaucrat. Miller also notes the impact of the Internet on new organizations. The Internet constitutes the nerve system that turns the vast number of churches in the developing world into a global *human* network. This network not only performs the obvious function of facilitating communication, but also the less obvious one of giving believers a sense of strength greater than their numbers, strictly considered, might warrant. With "everyone" seeming to be working and praying for the same goals at the same time, defeat is literally unimaginable.

I close with two observations prompted by my own work as a historian of Christianity in the United States. First, I worry about Miller's definition of Christian leadership (one schooled by his research on developing-world churches). "*Leadership within the Christian community,*" he tells us, "*involves, at its heart, helping individuals identify their callings as they commit themselves on a daily basis to discern what the Spirit of God is doing in the world.*" (18) This definition proves apt as far as it goes, but it underplays the role of a learned clergy, tutored by the accumulated wisdom of the church's life over the centuries. One of my senior colleagues—a superior instructor by any measure of such things—used to say that college teaching is not education by plebiscite. If students already knew what they are supposed to know, they would be the teachers. Something like the same principle applies to the church. Though notions of polity and ordination differ from one tradition to another, in the end, leaders must be more than discerners and enablers. They must prophetically bear "the hot coal of God's Word upon their lips and in their lives." A lofty responsibility it is, and not one readily gained outside a praying academy committed to exploring and thoughtfully applying the riches of the Christian tradition to the modern world.

The second observation is to say that we stand indebted to Professor Miller for his determination to take his subjects seriously. He has carefully and empathetically chronicled their behavior and, equally important, remained open to the possibility that they are telling the truth about miracles. Miller stands in good company; William James and Rudolf Otto did similarly. But by and large academic discourse these days implies, when it does not explicitly declare, that stories about God's extraordinary acts in history may be "meaningful" but not, really, "truthful." Miller's work reminds us that though the Enlightenment may form a decisive turning point in the Western tradition, it hardly constitutes the final word on its trajectory, let alone its end.

---

[11] See for example Elizabeth E. Brusco, *The Reformation of Machismo: Evangelical Conversion and Gender in Colombia* (Austin: University of Texas Press, 1995).

RADICAL CHALLENGE TO A PLODDING CHURCH

A Response by William H. Willimon, Professor of Christian Ministry and Dean of the Chapel Duke University, Durham, N.C.

I met sociologist Donald Miller through his fascinating study of "new paradigm churches," *Reinventing American Protestantism: Christianity in the New Millennium* (Berkeley: University of California Press, 1997). In that book, Miller provided a critique of North American Mainline Protestantism by looking at us through the lens of the burgeoning "new paradigm churches," those new congregations who, in the later part of the Twentieth Century, had become virtual international denominations through their unique mix of conservative, evangelical theology and innovative organizational and leadership structures.

Miller's paper, "Emergent Patterns of Christian Leadership" continues the approach that he pioneered in his earlier book. He views the Pentecostal explosion in Africa and South America from the standpoint of a North American Christian and finds important insights for the North American church.

I cannot adequately express the deep impact Miller's paper had upon me. As someone who has thought about, and prayed for, and worked in behalf of renewal of North American Mainline Protestant Christianity, Miller's paper struck me to the core and confirmed some of my own impressions. By the roving, creative work of the Holy Spirit, the center of Christianity is shifting to the South. The most interesting dynamism of the faith is to be found elsewhere than in my neighborhood or in my denomination.

There is an explosion taking place throughout Africa and South America. It is not being driven by Liberation Theology ("Liberation Theology embraced the poor and the poor embraced Pentecostalism"), nor is it taking as its model those comfortable and accommodated forms of the faith as practiced in the North. In its emphasis on "signs and wonders," its stress upon the miraculous and the power of the Holy Spirit, Pentecostalism represents a protest against much of the structures and the thought of the Christianity that produced and still characterizes my church. According to some church growth observers, nearly a third of the world's Christians are Pentecostal or charismatic. Most students of these matters regard Pentecostalism as the fastest growing segment of Christianity around the world.

Miller seems most interested in the communal and structural patterns that worldwide Pentecostalism produces. That is appropriate. He is a sociologist, after all. Some criticized Miller's earlier work for not examining the social impact, the political and social impact of these churches. The conventional charge against the Pentecostal resurgence is that it emphasizes spiritual transformation at the expense of social transformation. How well I remember the distinguished Liberation theologian who visited our seminary in the late Seventies saying, when asked about Pentecostalism in South America, "pie-in-the-sky, escapist theology is what the Pentecostals are about." Pentecostalism, according to this liberationist, was an attempt to leave the powers-that-be undisturbed. As observers like Miller have suggested, it was Liberation Theology, the last gasp of the Constantinian attempt to get a theological handle on the government, that was the accomodationist theology. Pentecostalism's challenge to the powers-that-be was much more radical and deep than neo-Marxist Liberation Theology.

As in my review of his book, even in this paper I found myself wanting to hear Miller talk more about the theological implications of his rather astonishing observations. His paper certainly stimulated my own thought on the theological implications of emergent Pentecostalism. What he describes strikes me as a profound challenge to the thought that has dominated our churches in the developed world. Liberation Theology, which presented itself as a challenge to the hegemony of the North and the West in the thinking and the structuring of the worldwide church, is exposed in this paper as one more way in which the church in the North continues to attempt to dominate the imagination of the church in the South.

Pentecostalism's stress upon the miraculous, for instance, strikes me as a deep and fundamental attack upon the way that Christianity has been presented to the West, at least since the 17th century. As Miller notes, here is Christianity moving from stress upon the message of the faith toward stress upon the actual experience of the faith. Or, as he put it in his book on the new paradigm churches, these churches stress the "medium" of the faith rather than the "message" of the faith. I wonder if it is more accurate to say that, in these churches, the medium – their free, adaptable, empowering structures of Christian experience – is their most interesting message. Miller's interest in the way these churches organize themselves and pioneer new structures of leadership and activity may be one of their great messages to the rest of us who are trapped in less productive, more self-protective modes of church polity.

Pentecostalism's stress upon the free, unconstrained movements of the spirit is a challenge to the way church life is conducted in my part of the world. What if the church is the result of the free, top down, giftedness of God rather than a product of our orderly, structured, hierarchical, essentially anthropological cultural patterns? In other words, Miller's paper is about as radical a challenge to the theology and practice of my safe, plodding, mainline church as I know.

In a review of Miller's book, I complained that he displayed too much sociological detachment from his subject and too little theological engagement. He appeared to want to ascribe the dramatic growth and surprising movements of these new paradigm churches to exclusively sociological factors. However, in this paper, although Miller's observations are presented as relatively objective, sociological observations on the leadership patterns of these churches in the developing world, one gets the distinct impression that Miller has "gone native," that he has come to embrace and to champion those theological tendencies which at one time he only observed with safe scientific detachment. That embrace is fine with me. I find the move of this California Episcopalian toward Third World Pentecostalism to be fascinating in itself, whatever the larger implications of his move may be. This is not some cool, detached, objective analysis of our situation. This is an impassioned confrontation with a mode of Christianity that is both an inspiration for and a judgement upon declining European and North American Christendom.

He says, "I did undergo a profound shift in my worldview when I realized that I was trapped in an Enlightenment ideology that privileged mind over body and perpetuated a dualistic epistemology that many of the postmodern members of new paradigm churches had long ago abandoned." Miller has, in this paper, embraced a postmodern consciousness and here presents the Pentecostal explosion in Africa and South America not only as a sociological phenomenon but also as an intellectual challenge.

I would encourage him to go a step further in his postmodernism and forsake the categories of modernists like Rudolph Otto in his analysis of Pentecostalism. Division of the world into the "natural" and the "supernatural," relegation of religious experience to the realm of some ethereal *mysterium tremendum* is a favorite ploy of the modern world to make religious experience irrelevant. I hope that his forthcoming *Pentecostalism and Social Transformation: A Global Analysis* will demonstrate a more postmodern recognition of the deep intellectual challenge that Pentecostalism presents to our Western, North American ways of apprehending the world. Modern thought forms, whether they knew it or not, were often attempts to exclude God from the world. They are therefore probably in need of abandonment if we are to think creatively about the signs and wonders being worked among us in the Pentecostal explosion. Miller seems to have embraced postmodernism when it comes to church structures, but not when it comes to theological reflection.

I do wonder about the implications of Miller's observations for those of us in mainline Protestantism. I find it difficult to conceive of how the Pentecostal experience can be folded into the experience of mainline Protestantism. Even though Miller was produced by mainline Protestantism, I sense too great a disjuncture between the theology and polity of these two wings of the church to believe that they can learn from one another. While the idea of North American congregations partnering with Pentecostal congregations in South America is exciting, I wonder if there are such vast differences of context and theology that such partnerships would be irrelevant. While I would pay good money to witness the deans of North American seminaries in conversation with Pentecostals in South America, I fear that the dialogue would be a waste of time for the Pentecostals. Perhaps I am demonstrating the limitations of my own essentially non-Pentecostal way of thinking. However, as Miller demonstrates, the Spirit of God is on the move throughout the world and, where the Spirit of God moves, there is always hope for change, threat of radical transformation, and promise of an outbreak of the Kingdom of God.